52

WINE WITH FOOD

Other Books by CYRIL RAY

Other book by ELIZABETH RAY

Wine With Food

by

CYRIL & ELIZABETH RAY

SIDGWICK & JACKSON
LONDON

We are grateful to Eric Chilman for kindly allowing us to reproduce
two of his poems, on pp. 17 and 22. They were originally
published in *Wine and Food*.

I.S.B.N. 0.283.98253.5

Printed in Great Britain by
A. Wheaton & Company, Exeter
for Sidgwick and Jackson Limited
1 Tavistock Chambers, Bloomsbury Way
London, W.C.1A 2SG

For Jonathan –
Our Other Joint Product

Contents

Note on the Drawings

AS IN three previous books of mine, the chapter-headings, decorative tail-pieces, and other drawings are from Bertall's *La Vigne: Voyage Autour des Vins de France*, published in Paris in 1878, which means that the author-artist was gathering his material in the wine-growing regions exactly a century ago.

I have turned to the same work yet again to illustrate a modest piece of my own – or, this time, partly of my own – because I should like to capture something of Bertall's light-hearted, though appreciative, attitude to a subject that is all too often, and especially in this country, approached too solemnly.

I wish only that my pen were as graceful as his pencil.

'BERTALL' is an anagram, or very nearly so, of one of the forenames of Charles Albert d'Arnoux (1820–1882), adopted as a pseudonym at the instance of Balzac, who was an early admirer of d'Arnoux, to whom he gave some of his work to illustrate.

D'Arnoux was a prolific illustrator and decorator, especially of children's books and magazines: *La Vigne* is the only major work I know of that he not only illustrated but wrote. He was a younger contemporary of Constantin Guys, Gavarni (with and for whom he worked) and Daumier.

He is a lesser draughtsman, but he shares something of their style, in economy of line and feeling for movement. In 1871, he was an anti-Communard when better artists than he – among them Courbet and Pissarro – sought to cherish, on the other side of the barricades, what the greatest of them all, Renoir, recognized as 'that little flame which never dies'.

C.R.

CHAPTER ONE

A Little of What
You Fancy . . .

A GREAT deal of rubbish is written about wine. I do not refer merely to such adventures of the soul among masterpieces as once were charted for the dons and the doctors, the St James's Street clubmen and the learned judges who, until a generation or so ago, largely composed the wine-buying classes – charted by literary gents confident that every historical allusion would be picked up and that no classical tag would need translation.

It was almost a century ago that Meredith wrote, in *The Egoist*, that

Of all our venerable British of the two Isles professing a suckling attachment to an ancient port-wine, lawyer, doctor, squire, rosy admiral, city merchant, the classic scholar is he whose blood is most nuptial to the webbed bottle. The reason must be, that he is full of the old poets. He has their spirit to sing with, and the best that Time has done on earth to feed it. He may also perceive a resemblance in the wine to the studious mind, which is the obverse of our mortality, and throws off acids and crusty particles in the piling of the

years until it is fulgent by clarity. Port hymns to his con-
servatism. It is magical: at one sip he is off swimming in the
purple flood of the ever youthful antique.

'Purple flood' is the phrase indeed for many such a passage
as Morton Shand's on claret, written in the 1920s (and I quote
only a part of it):

To compare the magnificent harmony of a fine Bordeaux to
a flight of alexandrines is to pay it a doubtful compliment...
for the genius of no great wine is less emphatic, declamatory
or monotonous. Grandeur it has, and in high degree, but I
find the 'scansion' of Bordeaux, if scansion there must be,
ranges from the Horatian to the Miltonic, from the rippling
lyrics of Herrick to the sway and surge of Swinburne in the
infinite variety of its scope; the 'rhythm' of its incarnadine
burden, the lilt of splendid majesty, never the din of rant
drowning the creaking of the buskins ...

Or Maurice Healy, opining just before the Second World
War that Clos de Vougeot would 'probably regard Cham-
bertin with the air that Marie Antoinette might have adopted
towards Mirabeau; it would acknowledge the ancient blood of
Romanée-Conti, without quite according the salute due to
Royalty; to Richebourg it would behave as Mrs Thrale towards Dr Johnson.'

That sort of writing about wine can be defended, and has had
its defenders.

Warner Allen (a classical scholar, as predicated by Meredith)
excused himself in the 1950s for having been guilty, a quarter of
a century before, of comparing a Pichon-Longueville 1899
with a Mouton of the same vintage in these terms:

'It had not quite the character of the Mouton nor its depth
and showed more of the superficiality of the silken fop, but it
was a courtier clothed in velvet with a finesse that left the enchanting memory of a dashing cavalier. Like Cyrano de
Bergerac, it had *panache*, a plume in its hat.'

He had been doing his best, he explained, 'to communicate
to someone who is as fascinated as I am by the elusively

delicate sensations produced by such a wine some idea of what that particular wine meant to me.'

Note, though, that whereas in the 1920s he had written that passage about *panache*, himself with *panache*, by the 1950s he felt obliged, if not to apologize, at any rate to explain what he now describes as 'indulging in a purple patch'.

For by the time his *Through the Wine Glass* appeared, in 1954, Raymond Postgate's *The Plain Man's Guide to Wine*, which had first appeared in 1951 (from the same publisher, interestingly enough), was already in its third impression. It gave the death-blow to the baroque style of writing about wine, and it is still, happily, in print.

Postgate, whose pupil I like to consider myself to have been, for I admired him more than anyone who has ever written about wine – a better classical scholar than Warner Allen, but one who believed that scholarship was not to be shown off but to be shared, and a Socialist who believed that so should be the good things of life – permitted himself no flight more fanciful than that sauternes should be taken 'in the right company – which is a plump, pretty and rather greedy young woman,' and then only after he had specified precisely with what dishes, immediately going on to explain that the wine in itself is syrupy but that fruit takes the edge off the sweetness, and then, in the simplest terms, what makes it sweet.

This is, indeed, plain writing for the plain man – commonsense about wine expressed in a commonsensible way.

Since Postgate's time, though, quite another sort of nonsense has come, not so much to be written (though it *is* sometimes written), but to a much greater extent talked, believed, and even *feared* about wine.

It is based on various closely related assumptions such as that there is some *mystery* about wine; that only men (and men rather than women) with a special, God-given, sense of taste can appreciate and understand it; that such-and-such a wine *must* be served with such-and-such a dish, at such-and-such a temperature; and that it is a breach of decorum to serve at any time and in any circumstances anything but the finest wine with a famous name, usually French or German.

Not only is this nonsense, but it is more harmful nonsense than the fancy fine writing that I made mock of in the opening paragraphs of this chapter. That, at any rate, conveyed or attempted to convey enjoyment.

The new nonsense inhibits enjoyment by raising such questions as, 'Am I doing the right thing?' 'Will my host (or my guest) despise me?' 'Am I enjoying this wine as much as I ought to enjoy it?'

(I suspect that for many people sex is not as much fun as it was before there were so many handbooks about it. I recently read somewhere that the tit-and-*tochas* magazines have driven more men to the psychiatrist's couch than to the whore's boudoir: they have been made to worry about their performance . . .)

The truth is – or the truths are – that:

There is no mystery about wine. It is the fermented juice of freshly gathered grapes – one of the oldest beverages known to man, one of the most natural and one of the most wholesome.

It is not meant to be a status symbol, but to be enjoyed, and anyone can enjoy it who can enjoy a glass of beer or a glass of lemonade; a slice of roast beef or a plate of fish and chips; a peach or an oyster.

Our sense of taste tells us how to savour such things; our sense of taste tells us how to savour a glass of wine. If it doesn't, don't drink it.

And whence, may I ask, comes the notion that women are less capable than men of appreciating and understanding wine? They ought to be – and potentially are – if anything, more capable. In this country, at any rate, men seem to be more heavily afflicted with bronchial and respiratory ailments than their wives and daughters, and these are afflictions that damage or diminish the sense of smell – and a sense of smell plays a large part in any consideration or appreciation of wine.

Women can choose or match a scent or a soap or a toilet-water more promptly and more surely than a man, just as they can taste a sauce or a soup in preparing dinner or say, more decisively than any man not professionally engaged, that this cushion clashes with those curtains, or that such a scarf would never do with such a frock.

A sense of smell, a sense of taste, and an eye for colour – most women have all these, to at least as great a degree as any man.

What they have lacked until our own time has been experience, because the economic and the social pattern of life in wine-drinking households has left women financially dependent on fathers or husbands, to whom it has fallen, therefore, to choose and to buy, to cellar and to serve the family's wines.

Now, at last, in this country, or so the statisticians say, more wine is bought by women than by men – thanks to the bulk shipping of cheap, branded wines and to the growth of supermarkets and self-service stores. The hand that reaches for the corn flakes brings home the burgundy. Splendid!

*　　*　　*

Perhaps this easy availability of sound, cheap wine will put an end to the apologies offered by nervous hosts for not serving a château-bottled claret or a late-gathered hock, where they would never apologize – why should they? – for not serving caviar, or smoked salmon, or pâté de foie gras, or oysters.

The pattern of wine-drinking in this country was laid down over the past couple of centuries by a leisured and learned – at any rate, moneyed – middle class when French, German, Spanish and Portuguese wine-growers lived simply and cheaply. The British wine-drinker was spoiled.

Now, we must get used to the fact that good wine is grown in North Africa and South America, as well as in Western Europe, and that swagger wines that have now reached an economic price are for swagger occasions.

How odd, meanwhile, that a host will apologize humbly for a perfectly respectable Chilean Cabernet or Yugoslav Traminer, whose wife, with a gracious smile, and not a hint of an apology, is serving frozen peas and bottled 'salad cream'.

*　　*　　*

To enjoy wine, as I have already suggested, what is needed is a sense of smell, a sense of taste and an eye for colour.

All else is experience and personal preference.

We all know the difference in taste and texture not only be-

tween fish and meat, but between mutton and beef, and between herring and halibut, because we have learned about food
by eating it.

(And sympathize, I beg you with the wretched wine-writer,
trying to explain the difference between claret and burgundy,
or between hock and sauternes, by imagining yourself putting
into words, to someone who has never eaten meat, the difference between the taste of beef and the taste of mutton ...)

Just as we learn about food by eating it, so we learn about
wine by drinking it – not by reading about it: not even in
books by me ...

And just as some people prefer beef to mutton, so some will
prefer burgundy, say, to claret.

It is a purely subjective choice: there is no moral judgement
involved and no nice point of etiquette. My wife likes her beef
underdone: I like the outside slice. She would choose a 1967 or
a 1969 claret, because she likes her red wines to have a little
crispness, a little edge, to them: I would choose a 1962, or even
a very much older one, for I like them soft, and full-blown.

(Some men like eighteen-year-old girls, some prefer thirty-
five-year-old women ...)

Neither of us is right, neither wrong.

So there are no rules about the drinking and serving of wine
such as might have been brought down by Moses, or laid down
by the more recently late Miss Mitford.

But as people have been drinking wine for thousands of
years, the very types we know today for many hundreds, there
is a certain amount of accumulated wisdom available – no, not
wisdom perhaps, but accumulated experience – that is worth
consulting before one goes one's own way.

Just as we know without trying, thanks to folk-memory,
that mustard goes well with roast beef but less well with baked
apples, that bacon and eggs is a more palatable combination
than kippers and strawberry jam, so our ancestors tell us that
red wine with fish leaves a sort of metallic taste in the mouth,
and that white wine is more refreshing if served approximately
cellar-cool, whereas red wine shows off its fragrance and its
fruitiness at room temperature.

All that this little book sets out to do is to enlarge upon these very general ideas in the light of Liz's experience and my own, for we have been lucky in having often been invited to travel widely through the wine-growing countries, to try this wine with that dish, sometimes to our delight and sometimes not . . .

But what neither of us would wish to do is to lay down the law. The only law there is about wine-drinking is that of the Abbey of Thélème – *Fay Ce Que Vouldras*. Or, to translate Rabelais's French into Marie Lloyd's English, a little of what you fancy does you good. . . .

There is no reason why we should not try for ourselves and, if we disagree with our great-grandfathers, drink our white wine tepid, our red wine with lumps of ice in it, and wash down *sole Normande* with vintage port.

Every anthology of English verse bears witness that Browning iced his claret and that Thackeray drank burgundy with bouillabaisse. Keats wrote in a letter of his liking for 'claret cool out of a cellar a mile deep', and sweet ratafia biscuits to go with it.

In our own time, John Christie not only had the taste to create Glyndebourne but the self-confidence to insist that only German wines should be served there – and only the sweetest at that. And Baron Philippe de Rothschild, at Château Mouton, where he makes what many people, including myself, regard as one of the greatest red wines of the world, and what some others, including Baron Philippe, regard as *the* greatest, drinks the great, sweet Château d'Yquem after dinner so heavily chilled that it has slivers of solid ice in the glass, which must drive the Marquis de Lur Saluces, who makes it, to tremble with rage . . .

I do not suggest that you follow the example either of the late Mr Christie or of Baron Philippe – merely to bear them in mind when you read our words on wine with food as re-minders that nothing that we say – or that anyone else says – about how or where or when to drink this wine or that needs to be paid any attention to at all. . . .

Only that when a particular wine and a particular dish and a particular person – as it might be you, dear reader – do hit it

off, time and place and loved one all together then, as a forgotten poet, Eric Chilman, sang to his lady:

> *Do I recall the night we met,*
> *With both our hearts* en feu?
> *As if I ever could forget,*
> *Dear* Cordon Bleu!
>
> *A lover's moon was in the sky.*
> *We dined alone, we twain.*
> Sole Véronique *was partnered by*
> *A still Champagne.*
>
> *You wore a bandeau on your hair,*
> *And with the* Coq au Vin
> *Produced a magnum old and rare*
> *Of Chambertin.*
>
> *Château d'Yquem, a last surprise,*
> *Was climax, crown and seal.*
> *I might forget your lovely eyes,*
> *But not that meal.*

CHAPTER TWO

The Wine When It Is Red

Bordeaux et bourgogne grand crus

WHEN the portrait-painter James Gunn lay dying, some seven or eight years ago, the Catholic priest by his bedside sought to comfort him by recounting the pleasures that awaited him in Paradise.

'Just imagine', he said, 'waking up in the company of all those good friends of yours, all good Catholics, all good talkers, all great wine-lovers – those old friends, Chesterton, Belloc and Baring, whom you painted in that famous Conversation Piece of yours . . .

'Just think, sitting there in the celestial sunshine, with good talk over good burgundy . . .'

The dying man opened one eye, and said, 'But, Father, I'm a claret man . . .'

*   *   *

Claret and burgundy, the two great red wines of France, not only remain the wines by which the world's red wines are judged, and in terms of which they are described, so that one says of this or that Australian or Algerian or Chilean wine that it is more like the one than the other, or the other than the one; but they are still compared and contrasted, as the examiners say.

So much so, as to convey the impression that they are radically *different* wines; that they are easily distinguishable from each other; and that any lover of wine must necessarily declare his allegiance to claret or to burgundy and, in that odiously cant phrase, stand up and be counted – I prefer, myself, to say 'nail his colours to the mast': after all, James Gunn went down with his flag flying . . .

It is, I think, much nearer to the truth to say that burgundy and claret – which is the red wine of Bordeaux – are two very similar wines, though with interesting differences that are usually, but by no means always, discernible by highly experienced tasters.

Mr Harry Waugh, formerly of Harveys of Bristol, now a director of the great first-growth claret, Château Latour, and a legendary character in the wine trade for his skill and judgement as a taster, was once asked whether he had ever mistaken a burgundy for a claret, and ruefully replied, 'Not since luncheon'.

Not every wine runs true to form: there are clarets that approximate to burgundy in style, and some burgundies – though I fancy there are fewer – that could pass as clarets.

In my salad days, when I was green in judgement, I used roundly to declare that I was a burgundy man, the fact of the matter being that that was in the 1930s when I was living on a *Manchester Guardian* salary of five and a half guineas a week, and my flat-mate and I used to buy only wine that was two shillings a bottle or less.

The burgundy – or what passed as burgundy – that could be bought at that sort of price was easier to drink than what was generally supposed to be claret, at two bob a bottle.

Cheap burgundy, especially before the laws of *appellation* came to be applied here, or even seriously to bite in France, was smooth and fruity, perhaps sugared a little – who knows? – but it was easy to drink, and didn't half impress various young women with our worldliness and wealth. It even softened some of them into malleability . . .

Cheap clarets, on the other hand, tended to be thinner, more acid, less immediately attractive, and it was only when, on my way to the war, I was living in London, on every penny of eight pounds a week (the *Manchester Guardian*, notoriously open-handed, felt that a war correspondent should be paid for the risks he ran), and could occasionally afford seven or eight shillings a bottle, that I came to know and to like the single-vineyard clarets.

Now, all I will say is that when each is most typically itself it is claret that appeals to me more, though I have drunk noble burgundies in my time: but then good claret is easier to come across than good burgundy; it is cheaper; I have drunk more claret than I have burgundy; and I have visited Bordeaux more often than I have visited Beaune, and have more friends there.

And, finally, that all this is subjective: I would not seek to say that claret is better than burgundy, only that it is different, and that the difference is such as to make it claret that is more to my taste.

Beyond that, I can do no better than to quote Eric Chilman's *Bordeaux, Bourgogne:*

> '*Claret is king.*'
>   '*Not so! For me*
> *The king of wines is Burgundy,*
> *The puissant and royal wine*
> *That dukes of the Burgundian line*
> *Drank once in Dijon.*'
>
>   '*How you gloat*
> *On treasures of your Golden Côte,*
> *Your Nuits, your Beaune! Therein we see,*
> *I grant you, high nobility,*
> *But balance,* nuance, *these are found*
> *On Bordelais, not Burgundian ground.*
> *Claret is king.*'
>
>   '*What can you see*
> *In Claret's puny subtlety*
> *To rival Bourgogne's robe, its strong*
> *Savour of sun and vintage song?*
> *Bourgogne is king.*'
>   '*Nonsense! Bordeaux!*'

'A certain courtesy we owe
In vinous argument.'
  'Agreed.'
'Then let us give each wine its meed,
Which compromise I take to mean
That one is king, the other queen.
You differ?'
  'Rather I divine
A Dual Monarchy of Wine.'

★   ★   ★

Writers about wine usually try to indicate the difference between the two wines – I have done it myself, often enough – by
suggesting that claret is the wine for roasts and grills and cold
meats rather than for game and rich stews, for which burgundy
is more suitable.

Now, I would rather say that although I think claret with
cold beef or a cold grouse is just about the perfect luncheon
combination, whenever you can drink claret you can drink
burgundy, and t'other way round. And with clarets I class the
excellent Cabernet wines of Chile.

With rich stews, game, and other highly flavoured meat
dishes, there is more to be said, I think, for the heavier wines of
the Rhône, such as Châteauneuf du Pape and Hermitage, for
the bigger Italian wines, such as Barolo and the *riserva* Chiantis,
and for the hearty wines of Tunisia and Morocco.

It is sheer bad luck that the red wines of Algeria – the biggest
wine-producing country in the world, after Italy, France and
Spain – are still under a cloud in this country, though they are
always cheap, and often good.

It seems that after the fall of France, many French ships on
the high seas carrying wine from Algiers to France and other
overseas markets put into British ports, and by December 1940
there was lying in our dock warehouses a hundred times as
much Algerian wine as Britain had imported per year before
the war.

What to do with a hundred years' supply of Algerian wine?
H.M. Customs, whose problem it was, insisted that it be

labelled 'Produce of North Africa' or 'Produce of Algeria', but it all went like hot cakes, and there were no complaints during the otherwise lean years of 1940 to 1944. The head of a firm of London wine-shippers, who was consulted at the time, tells me that the red wines were very good – 'very high alcoholic strength, enormous body and flavour' – probably ordered by French exporters to blend with the inferior wines of the Midi. The white wines were disappointing, having oxidized in the warehouses, but were sold to make vermouth – quite successfully.

It was after the war that the trouble arose. British experts went to Algiers after it had been liberated, but before France was completely free, to select wines that would be part of a barter deal between British and French governments, and again the first shipments were welcomed everywhere. But when France itself was freed, many shippers preferred to wait until it was possible again to import clarets and burgundies and did not take up their quotas of Algerian, which lay in the warehouses, deteriorating in cask, because of lack of skilled attention in the way of topping up and sulphuring, long after they should have been bottled.

Now whether it was that one or two interested firms began a whispering campaign against the Algerian wine, or that some of the spoiled wine did reach the British market and disappoint post-war wine-drinkers, who now had good French wine with which to make comparisons, I do not know. What does seem certain is that quite a lot of Algerian wine was drunk and enjoyed in this country until thirty years ago, and that its unfortunate reputation dates from no longer ago than that.

On the whole, then, I suggest claret or burgundy, according to taste, with pretty well any meat dish; and the fuller-bodied reds, from the Rhône, from the Rioja region of Spain, from some parts of Italy, and from any part of north Africa, with the richest meats.

There are red wines that are lighter in body and in flavour even than clarets, such as those of the Italian lakes – Valpolicella and Bardolino – that are delicious with cold meats, with chicken and the like. The people who grow them drink them cellar-cool, which is how many people drink their new Beaujolais – Beaujolais *primeur*, or *nouveau*, or *de l'année*, for which there is such a vogue these days.

(There is a local saying, that a young Beaujolais should be '*bu, pissé et payé avant Paques*'.)

The vogue has been overdone, as these things always are, but a good young Beaujolais (after a sunless summer, as in 1973, they can be very acid), drunk within six months or so of the vintage, is mouth-filling in its fruitiness, yet deliciously re-freshing, a wine to be gulped, and a good companion to the softer, runnier cheeses, like those of Normandy, Champagne and the Ile de France – Brie and Camembert and the less highly regarded but, in consequence, less often imitated, Carré de l'Est.

Cheese is wine's best friend, for cheese is to milk what wine is to the grape. But as kinds of cheese are as many and as varied as are the kinds of wine, the permutations and combinations are endless.

Clarets and burgundies go beautifully with hard or crumbly, white and red, English cheeses, such as Cheddar and Cheshire, Lancashire and Leicester and Wensleydale; the bigger wines, such as I have suggested as partners for game, with blue cheeses from home or abroad – Stilton or Roquefort or Gorgonzola.

With Danish Blue you may serve Coca-Cola, so far as I am concerned, for I will neither drink the one nor eat the other. And I do not speak of those winsome little triangles in silver paper, for I speak of cheese . . .

Ben Gunn – no relation of the character with whom I opened this chapter, but the castaway in *Treasure Island* – con-demned to a diet of coconuts, said that, 'Many's the long night I've dreamed of cheese – toasted, mostly', and in his position I should have dreamed of Guinness, too . . .

And let no one suppose that because cheese and wine are natural partners, and because it is the English tradition to drink port with Stilton, then port may be poured *into* a Stilton. When Stilton needs moistening, it needs throwing away.

Liz

Ray says that he likes cold beef and claret, and his favourite form of cold beef is *Boeuf à la Mode*, which, unlike the Sunday joint, is cooked specially to be eaten cold. This is a good dish for a party, as it has to be made well in advance, so that the jelly with which the meat is covered has time to set. Any jelly to spare can be used as a cold soup, or for *oeufs en gelée*.

BOEUF À LA MODE

Season and brown in oil a three-pound piece of beef – unsalted silverside, top-side, or a similar cut. Put it into a casserole when it is browned, and in the same pan sauté three onions and two or three carrots until the onions look transparent, then add to the beef, together with some salt, garlic, bay-leaf and thyme, and a dessertspoonful of tomato purée. Add two pigs' trotters that have been split lengthways, and cover the whole with half water, half red wine. Put the lid on the casserole and cook in a gentle oven (300° gas 1) for four or five hours.

When cooked, remove the meat and let it cool under a weight. Strain the liquid into a bowl and let it get cold, so that the fat can be easily removed. Slice the meat when cold and pour over the liquid, which will cover the meat with a soft jelly. The beef can be garnished with freshly cooked carrots, and little heaps of the jelly to which some chopped parsley has been added.

Beef, 3lb; onions, 3; carrots, 3; pigs' trotters, 2; garlic; thyme; bay-leaf; salt; pepper; tomato purée; red wine; water; oil

A good hot dish to go with red wine is made with lamb, and as it is north Italian in origin, it goes well with such Italian wines as Bardolino or Valpolicella – but just as well, of course, with Beaujolais or claret.

SGUAZETO ALLA FRIULANA

Cut two and a half pounds of lean lamb into pieces, heat some butter and oil in a pan, add a tooth of garlic, a finely chopped onion, a little pork fat cut into dice, and cook until the onion softens. Add the pieces of lamb, season with salt, pepper, and a pinch of cinnamon. Brown the meat well, turning it frequently, so that it cooks evenly. Dilute a tablespoon of tomato paste with enough stock to cover the meat, cover and cook very slowly on top of the stove for about two hours, until the meat is very tender and the sauce thick.

Lamb, 2½lb; garlic; onion; pork fat; butter and oil; salt; pepper; cinnamon; tomato purée; stock

One of the best-known dishes to use red wine in the making is *coq au vin*, and here is a version made with Beaujolais rather than one of the heavier reds.

COQ AU BEAUJOLAIS

Joint a chicken and brown the pieces in a mixture of oil and butter. Add two rashers of diced bacon, two onions and a tooth of garlic all finely chopped. When these are all brown pour over them a bottle of Beaujolais, season with salt, pepper and a *bouquet garni*. Bring the sauce rapidly to the boil for a minute or two to reduce the wine a little, then cover the pan and cook gently either over a low heat on top of the cooker, or in a very moderate oven for about three-quarters of an hour. Then add two dozen small pickling onions and continue the cooking until they and the chicken are quite cooked. (The easiest way to skin the onions is to pour boiling water over them for a moment or two, when the skins can be taken off quite simply.) Have ready some *beurre manié*, by mixing together an ounce of butter with the same amount of flour and rolling into marble-sized balls (used to thicken stews and casseroles).

When the chicken is ready, remove the pieces, together with the onions and bacon, and keep warm on a serving dish. To the sauce remaining in the pan add the *beurre manié*

gradually, stirring carefully over a moderate heat until the
sauce thickens, then pour it over the chicken.

*Chicken, 1; onions, 2; bacon rashers, 2; garlic, 1 tooth; pickling
onions, 24; salt; pepper; beurre manié, 2oz; Beaujolais, 1
bottle; oil; butter*

Another famous red wine dish is Boeuf Bourguignon, which,
as the name tells us, originates in Burgundy, although it can be
made successfully with red wines from other parts. It is similar
to the chicken dish above, but made with beef instead.

Game goes well with red wine, of course, either cooked in it
or eaten with it, but game is seldom with us, and expensive
when it is. Pigeon, though, which Ray calls the poor man's
partridge, is available all year round, and very good eating:
why is it used so little? Pigeons are shot as vermin, and often
not even collected but left on the ground to rot. If there is a
local farmer who shoots pigeons, offer to pay for his cartridges,
and you will have a bargain. When cooking pigeon, allow at
least one bird each, as there is not a great deal of meat except
for the breast. However, one way of using them is to use the
breasts for a salmi, saving the other bits of meat from the legs,
to be minced with butter and a little brandy and put into a
terrine as a delicious pâté.

SALMI OF PIGEON

Take six pigeons (for four people). Mix some butter with
salt, nutmeg, pepper and ginger and put a good lump of this
seasoned butter inside each bird. Arrange the birds breast
down in a well buttered casserole, dot with more butter – the
birds tend to be a bit dry, so need plenty of butter (or
chicken fat if you have it) – cover with foil and the lid of the
casserole, put this into a slow oven for about two hours, or
until the meat is quite tender.

When they are cooked there will be a good deal of
buttery liquid in the casserole – use some of this to make a
sauce, and keep the rest to mix with the pigeon trimmings
for the pâté.

For the sauce, dice an onion and soften in butter, then add a little of the pigeon liquid and a glass of red wine, a bayleaf, salt, pepper, a pinch of herbs and a dessertspoonful of red currant jelly. Let this simmer for half an hour while you take the breast meat off the pigeons in two neat pieces. Heat these thoroughly in the sauce and thicken with a little arrowroot. Put on to a serving dish and garnish with triangles of fried bread.

Pigeons, 6; butter; salt; pepper; nutmeg; ginger; bayleaf; onion; red wine; redcurrant jelly; arrowroot

Another neglected wild meat is rabbit, also available all year round. One way to cook it is with mustard, which gives a piquant flavour to the dish without being hot. Traditionally, this should be Dijon mustard, and the dish goes well with the wines of nearby Burgundy and Beaujolais.

LAPIN À LA MOUTARDE
(OR LAPIN DIJONNAIS)

Joint a good-sized rabbit, and cook in butter until the pieces are well coloured. Pour a glass of brandy over them and light it, shaking the pan until the flame dies down. Spread the rabbit joints with a good coating of Dijon mustard, then put them into a fire-proof dish. Chop an onion and soften this in the same pan in which the rabbit was browned and then put in half a pound of mushrooms. Cook the onion and mushrooms for a few minutes then add a little stock and a quarter-pint of cream. Mix this sauce well, pour it over the rabbit joints and bake in a medium oven for an hour and a half. Cook covered for the first hour, then remove the lid for the rest of the time. Serve in the dish in which it was cooked.

Rabbit, 1; brandy, 1 glass; mustard; onion, 1; mushrooms, $\frac{1}{2}$lb; stock; cream, $\frac{1}{4}$ pint

Another good example of how savoury mustard can be without being merely hot is this mustard tart. Very likely it came from Dijon also or some other mustard-making part of France, but I came upon it first at Portmeirion, that enchanting Italianate village in north Wales, that has become a refuge for the Ray family from the trials, tribulations and telephone calls of modern life. As will be seen, it is a piquant sort of quiche or savoury flan.

TARTE À LA MOUTARDE

Line an open flan case with ½lb short crust pastry, and bake it 'blind' for about 15 minutes at 400° gas 6. Remove from the oven and leave to cool. Remove the skins and pips from five tomatoes, and cut them in half. When the flan case is cool cover the base with a layer about one-eighth of an inch thick of French mustard, sprinkle over this 4oz grated Gruyère cheese, and on this place the halved tomatoes. Beat two egg yolks with 2oz cream and pour this mixture over the flan. Bake in a slow oven (250° gas 1) for about half an hour.

Shortcrust pastry, ½lb; Gruyère cheese, 4oz; tomatoes, 5; cream, 2oz; egg yolks, 2; French mustard

So far, these recipes have been mainly associated with Burgundy – not unnaturally, as this part of France is noted for its devotion to good food. More so than the country round Bordeaux, although, to my mind anyway, the Bordeaux wines are finer than the burgundies. However, there are some good dishes from the Bordeaux region, particularly of lamb, as the salt marshes nearby provide good *pre-salé* meat. First, though, a good soup, different from the onion soup usually found in France.

POTAGE TOURIN

Melt two ounces of butter in a saucepan, slice half a pound of onions thinly and cook them in the butter until they are transparent, but not brown. Sprinkle with a tablespoon of flour, stir well, then pour in a pint or slightly more of hot milk, season well with salt and pepper, turn the heat down and simmer for about a quarter of an hour. Just before serving beat two egg yolks with three tablespoons of cream, pour this mixture into the soup and stir to thicken but do not let it boil or it may curdle. It is easier to pour a little of the hot soup on to the eggs and cream to mix, then add this to the saucepan, rather than putting the eggs in straightaway. Dry slices of French bread in the oven, put a slice at the bottom of each soup plate and pour the hot soup over.

Onions, ½lb; butter, 2oz; flour, 1 tablespoon; milk, 1¼ pints; salt; pepper; egg yolks, 2; cream, 3 tablespoons; French bread

One of the customs in this part of the country is to '*faire chabrot*' which means that when the last of the bread is eaten a glass of red wine is poured into the remaining drops of soup and drunk from the plate.

GIGOT À LA BORDELAISE

For a five-pound leg of lamb take three-quarters of a pint of wine vinegar, or a mixture of red wine and vinegar. Bring this to the boil with three or four teeth of garlic in it. Put the leg into a hot oven (450° gas 8) for fifteen minutes, then reduce the heat to 350° gas 4. Cook the lamb for an hour and a half, basting frequently with the vinegar mixture.

Leg of lamb, 5lb; vinegar, or vinegar and red wine, ¾ pint; garlic, 3 teeth

This is also the part of France for a distinctive type of fungus called *cèpes*. They are brown and flat, sometimes as big as plates. They have a curious resilient texture, and you either like them very much or not at all. I like them, Ray doesn't. This is a typical way of cooking them, and big field mushrooms can be treated the same way.

CÈPES À LA BORDELAISE

Wipe the *cèpes* or mushrooms clean, remove the stems but reserve them. Cook the sliced *cèpes* in hot oil for a few minutes until brown, then lower the heat and cook gently for about twenty minutes. Pour off most of the oil, season with salt and pepper and cook again until the slices stiffen, then keep hot in a serving dish. Put a couple of tablespoons of fresh oil into the pan, chop the stalks with two shallots and when the oil is hot put them into the pan and cook for a few minutes. Return the sliced *cèpes* to the pan and mix all together. Sprinkle with salt, parsley and a little lemon juice and serve very hot.

Cèpes, or field mushrooms, 1lb; oil; shallots, 2; parsley; lemon juice; salt; pepper

The cooking of the Bordeaux region has been much influenced by Périgord, to the east, and particularly by the Basque country, to the south, with dishes like the strangely named *chipirons* (which is a kind of squid), smoked ham from Bayonne, and small spicy sausages. Many dishes from this area depend too much on local materials for us to be able to use them easily, but this Basque dish is a sort of French version of a Spanish omelette and makes a good light supper or lunch dish, or can be served as a first course.

PIPERADE

Slice a large onion finely, and cook in oil until it begins to soften. Add three sliced green peppers (remove the seeds carefully first) and cook for about fifteen minutes until they are nearly soft. Add a pound of tomatoes, skinned and roughly chopped. Season with salt, pepper, a little parsley or marjoram and cook gently until all the vegetables are soft but not mushy. Lower the heat and pour six well-beaten eggs over the vegetables, stirring as for scrambled eggs, but don't let them get too solid. Serve with ham or bacon, or just with fried croutons.

Large onion, 1; green peppers, 2–3; tomatoes, 1lb; oil; salt; pepper; parsley or marjoram; eggs, 6

Another oddity about the Bordelais is the devotion to Dutch cheese. This seems to date from the days when wine was shipped to the Netherlands, and the ships brought back Dutch cheeses as ballast (there is a lot of Bath stone in the area too, having come from Bristol as ballast). Cheese goes particularly well with red wine, and although I find Dutch cheese rather too bland, it is a good companion to the red wines of the Bordeaux area. Cooked cheese dishes, too, go well, and one of the simplest and best known of all cheese dishes is, of course, Welsh Rabbit. (You will make Ray very cross if you call it 'rarebit'.) Everyone has a special version – here is one:

WELSH RABBIT (for four)

Warm three tablespoons of milk in a saucepan and add half a pound of grated cheese and let it melt slowly into the milk. Season with pepper, a little salt, a pinch of dry mustard, and a dash of Worcester sauce. When the cheese has melted, add the yolks of three eggs, stir them into the cheese until the mixture has thickened. Pour over hot buttered toast, put under a hot grill until it begins to bubble, and serve at once.

Milk, 3 tablespoons; cheese, ½lb; salt; pepper; mustard; Worcester sauce; egg yolks, 3; toast, 4 slices

Another way of cooking cheese that is good for any meal, including breakfast if you feel strong enough to eat at all at that time of day, is to make aigrettes, known more simply in our family as Cheese Blobs. They can be eaten as they are, with mustard sauce, or with rolls of crisp bacon.

CHEESE AIGRETTES

Put an ounce of butter into half a pint of water, seasoned with salt and cayenne pepper. Bring this to the boil then add, all in one go, four ounces of flour, stirring all the time while the flour cooks and becomes a thick mass. Stir in three ounces of grated cheese, remove the pan from the fire and beat in two eggs, one at a time, stirring the first one until it is absorbed before adding the second. This makes a thick springy paste, which you let cool. When ready to be served, make some oil very hot in a deep pan. Drop in spoons of the mixture, frying until they are brown outside. Drain well before serving hot, while they are crisp outside but soft within.

Butter, 1oz; water, ¼pint; cayenne; salt; flour, 4oz; eggs, 2; cheese, 3oz; oil for frying

Finally, a word about puddings that are relevant to red wine. In the picturesque town of St Emilion, just north of Bordeaux, every shop sells macaroons, each one claiming to be the *veritable* version. Here is one, certainly *veritable*, as it was given to me by Madame Querre of Château Monbousquet, where they grow fine wine.

ST ÉMILION MACAROONS

Mix well together half a pound of ground almonds and ten ounces of sugar. Beat the whites of five eggs until stiff and fold into the almond mixture. Drop small spoonfuls of this on to a baking tray lined with oiled foil or rice paper and bake in a slow oven for twenty minutes, when they should be a delicate brown. Allow plenty of room between the macaroons as they tend to spread in the cooking.

Ground almonds, ½lb; caster sugar, 10oz; egg whites, 5

One way of serving these delicacies from a red-wine region is as an accompaniment to pears cooked in red wine.

POIRES RICHELIEU

Peel six ripe pears, leave them whole and poach in half a bottle of light red wine, with two ounces of sugar, a pinch of cinnamon and the grated rind of an orange. When cooked, remove to a serving dish. Add two or three tablespoons of redcurrant jelly to the wine and boil it up to reduce and thicken a little. Pour this over the pears and serve cold, with whipped cream and macaroons. Peaches can be cooked the same way.

Pears, 6; red wine, ½ bottle; sugar, 2oz; redcurrant jelly, 2–3 tablespoons; cinnamon; grated orange rind

Bourgogne et charentes

CHAPTER THREE

Sweet and Dry

THERE are those, and I am not one of them, who accept the convention, 'red wine with meat, white wine with fish', but make an exception in favour of red wine with salmon, red mullet, and lampreys – the first two because the fish are themselves red-fleshed or, at any rate, pinkish; lampreys because they are usually cooked in red wine (and their own blood).

For myself, I accept only half the convention, but that is the half that counsels white wine with fish, for I find that fish washed down with red leaves a tinny taste in the mouth – and that this is as true, for me, of salmon and red mullet as it is of herring and halibut.

As for lampreys, I am in no danger of dying of a surfeit, for I was put off them for life merely by making their acquaintance in the great, round, mouth-wateringly marvellous market of Bordeaux, the revolting reptiles baring their fangs at me in baleful leers.

(Is this what has put the English off an English fish, or is it because a lust for them killed an English king? Some scholars hold that the French word *lamproie* derives from the English, not the other way round; the Thames used to teem with them, and the Severn still does, or did until very recently – potted lamprey was on sale as a local delicacy in shops at Worcester and Cheltenham until well within living memory, and there are old English recipes for cooking them in cider – presumably from Herefordshire.

Come to that, what has happened to the potted char one used to be able to buy in the village shops of England's Lakeland? 'With a char on the table' – I quote from a century-old gourmet's guide – 'worthy associate of Wordsworth and Southey, and with Windermere and Rydal Mount in view, we are truly in the heart of the Lake Poetry.'

No one nowadays, it seems, bothers to catch and to pot the char, yet it is the same fish as the *omble chevalier* for which English visitors pay vast prices in the Michelin-starred restaurants on the shores of Lake Annecy.)

★   ★   ★

I think there is some scientific – chemical? – reason for the metallic taste I mention that seems to me, as to others, to arise from a combination of fish and red wine, and I observe the convention not for convention's sake but for comfort's.

There is no such reason for outlawing white wine with meat. Indeed, Stephen Gaselee, who died a generation ago, a great scholar not only of Coptic texts and of Latin of the silver and of the middle ages, but also of food and drink, took chablis with his chops, and thanked God for it in his *Grace During Meat*:

> *On china blue my lobster red*
> *Precedes my cutlet brown,*
> *With which my salad green is sped*
> *By yellow Chablis down.*
>
> *Lord, if good living be no sin,*
> *But innocent delight,*
> *O polarize these hues within*
> *To one eupeptic white!*

Neither so pious nor so scholarly as Sir Stephen, I almost invariably serve red wine myself with meat, but that is because I like red wine – even if I have served a white wine with a main course of fish, I like at least a mouthful of red with a morsel of cheese to follow, or the meal seems unfinished.

Many dry white wines that are delightfully fresh and crisp with fish – how superlatively good is Muscadet with oysters or with mussels, or the local Soave with a Venetian fish-fry! – are rather light in body and, as it were, in texture, to go with a richly savoury meat dish. Others that I can enjoy with fish, especially fish in sauces that have a touch of sweetness about them, such as *sole Véronique* – wines, that is, such as hocks and other rieslings, or white Graves – are to my taste a little too sweet for roasts and grills and stews.

Some time, though, I must try a full-flavoured hock with oxtail *des vignerons*, which Liz makes when the sweet little green Cyprus dessert grapes are cheap here and plentiful, by stewing the oxtail in them and their juice. A subtle sweetness underlies the rich heartiness of the splendid dish, and I think a white wine with a similar hint of sweetness, served cool, might be just the thing.

The last of my reasons for not serving white wine with meat is that the one that would go very well with a steak or a sirloin or a saddle, if not with stews or with game, is white burgundy which, at its best, has great character and depth of flavour. It would have to be a white burgundy of fine quality, though, and wines of that sort are as dear as, or dearer than, the grandest clarets – today (or, as the new breed of *Times* leader-writer would put it, 'at this moment in time') a Corton Charlemagne ready to drink costs a tenner, which is as much as a 1966 first-growth claret, and Le Montrachet twice as much.

More modest white burgundies would probably not have the body, whereas very much more modest red burgundies would do very well.

All this, though, is one man's individual taste, and an Englishman's at that. In the wine-growing regions, they drink their own wines in their own way.

Liz and I were once entertained to luncheon at one of the

great first-growth châteaux of Barsac, famous even among its noble neighbours for the golden glory of its luscious wine. Other guests were some of the most noted sweet-wine growers of Barsac and Sauternes.

With each course came a wine of the region bigger and sweeter than the last until, with the gigot of salt-marsh mutton roasted over vine branches, we were drinking that honey-sweet and scented miracle, Château d'Yquem 1921.

I forebore to comment, for I was wondering how my liver was going to cope with so cloying a meal, and thinking how much more I could have enjoyed the fabulous wine with a meltingly ripe peach, and how much more happily the mutton would have marched with a bottle of claret from only just the other side of Bordeaux.

Our host, though, had been expecting compliments, and he broke in with, 'Don't you think our white wines here are very pretty?'

Oh yes, indeed I did, I assured him; oh yes, indeed . . .

My host had known, he said, that I would agree with him: he inclined his head in a courteous gesture towards my connoisseurship.

'What do you think', he said, 'of those fellows in the Médoc, drinking that sour red wine of theirs?'

The Médoc is a good thirty miles away.

Geography and parochial pride set the pattern of wine-drinking in France, and meals of that sort are common in the Sauternais, where they drink their rich sweet wines with *pâté de foie gras des Landes* in the middle of a meal, on the principle of rich with rich, where most of us would choose to cut the richness of the liver with a much more sharply dry wine.

(Even the red-wine growers of the Bordelais drink sauternes with the local truffled goose-liver, perhaps believing that no claret is rich enough . . .)

A banquet given at Château d'Yquem itself in 1926 'was considered', according to the classic French work on the wines of the region, 'quite perfect, and is still quoted as a model of its kind'.

After a 1904 Château Filhot, also a renowned sweet white

wine, a 1914 Yquem accompanied a rich dish of langouste; a
1921 Yquem the ducks' wings roasted in an orange sauce; and
an 1869 Yquem the cold fillets of beef in a glazed sauce of
truffles, pâté de foie gras and red wine.

'Notice', the good book goes on, 'that the three Château
d'Yquems are great vintages: the 1914 not so rich and luscious
as the celebrated 1921 and 1869, but very fine and elegant all
the same.'

So the wines became more lusciously sweet as the dishes
became richer . . .

The 1921 Yquem was a young wine then, and became a
legend. I have drunk it twice since the day when it washed
down my roast mutton in the Sauternais, but on both occasions
in England and with fruit, so that it went down more com-
fortably.

What I remember best about it, though, is the story I was
told by a girl I knew, early in the war, who had recently been
divorced, and greatly to her surprise, by her much older and,
hitherto, complaisant husband:

They had lived, she and the husband, in a stately Sussex
home, the park of which had been turned by the War Office
into a tented field, and its greater rooms into the officers' mess
of a smart and rather rakish regiment.

Its subalterns were not indifferent to the lady's charms; the
lady herself not unduly prim, nor hard to please. It was some-
how understood that neither the colonel nor the cuckolded
husband would complain, so long as certain decencies – or, to
be more precise, certain reticences – were observed.

And yet . . . the blow fell. The lady and that evening's
lover were discovered, when on other evenings with other
young men her adventures had gone carefully unnoticed. She
was turned out into the black-out at little more than a moment's
notice, and divorced as quickly as a lady could.

It was long before she could understand why, she told me.
Why that evening, and not on any other? And then it had
dawned on her. Until that particular evening, she had dis-
pensed her favours, by previous and prettily planned arrange-
ment, in boudoir or in bedroom. It was an understood thing,

and the eyes both of martial and of marital authority had
winked at it. But on the particular, the fatal, evening she was
showing off the house to a recently joined young officer, and
they had reached the wine cellar which, in that house, was
very properly a show-place. A look in his hostess's eye overwhelmed the boy; his ardour would not wait; and they were
heard, and thus discovered, in such a position, she shyly in-
timated, as to be agitating the bin of Yquem 1921.

The husband was unduly hasty. Had he stopped to think, he
would have remembered that white wines – even a twenty-
year-old dessert wine – throw no deposit, or none to speak of,
and shaking does them little harm. Now, had it been a bin of
the 1920 Lafite (the great 1920 clarets were delicious drinking
well into the 1960s) he would have been justified in having his
wife dragged naked through the streets at the cart's tail, and
slitting her lover's weazand . . .

*   *   *

To talk of Yquem and the like, though, is to talk of the
grandees of the unfortified sweet wines (as distinct from port
and the like, which have brandy added to them, to arrest
fermentation). The great German *beerenauslesen* and *trocken-
beerenauslesen* are of the same full, heavy, character – perhaps
better drunk by themselves, very cool, in glasses bigger than
those in which one would serve port, but not in much greater
quantities: the glass only about a third full, so that one can dip
one's nose into the honey-sweet smell of the golden wine . . .

When wines of this breeding become very old, they retain
great depth of flavour and bouquet and, although still sweet, or
sweetish, lose a great deal of their cloying lusciousness.

At this late stage in their development, so long as they have
not become *madérisé* – turned brown in colour and in taste, that
is, like madeira, through oxidization, as old white wines often
do – such great sweet wines are served by some connoisseurs
with smoked salmon. The wines are 'big' enough to comple-
ment the oily, smoky, salty fish, and the lemon and black
pepper that go with it.

An interesting idea, and palatable, but not my own choice.

*   *   *

The advantage that white wines have over red is that there is a greater range.

To go with fish, there are dry wines such as the Soave and the Muscadet I have already mentioned, to say nothing of Verdicchio, from Italy's Adriatic coast, and the rieslings of Alsace, which are drier than those from the other side of the Rhine because they are more fully fermented out.

Of the German wines, though, those from the Mosel, Saar and Ruwer, in their green bottles, are lighter and drier than the Rhine wines, in brown.

And if, dear reader, you want to know why Rhine wine (though not the Mosels) is known in English-speaking countries as 'hock', here is the story as told to us by a Rhine-wine-grower with whom we took a glass one sunny morning on the terrace of the Swann at Oestrich, on the right bank of the busy river, and in the middle of its greatest vineyards.

'Your Queen Victoria', he said, 'visited these parts in 1850' (which, indeed, she did: the books confirm it) 'and she was particularly taken with the wines of Hochheim, just upstream and round the bend from here . . .'

(Sure enough, she gave permission for a vineyard there to be named after her, the Koenigen Viktoria Berg: to this day, its wine bears an exuberant high-Victorian label, all gold medals and quarterings, and a picture of the tower erected among the vines to commemorate the visit.)

'And she liked Germany so much', said our guide, 'and the wines of Germany, and especially those of Hochheim, that every time she sat down to dine she used to raise her glass and cry' (here he threw his own head back, lifted his own glass, and raised his own voice) '. . . your good Queen Victoria used to raise her glass, and cry, "A bottle of hoc' keeps away the doc'."'

Never mind that the Oxford English Dictionary derives it, by way of 'hockamore' – which is to say Hochheimer – all the way back to 1625: hard fact has spoiled many a good story . . .

★   ★   ★

The Mosels and the drier hocks go well with fish; the fuller, fruitier hocks even with such rich German meat dishes as chine of venison in cream-and-cranberry sauce.

So most Rhinelanders maintain: some Germans and more Englishmen find the typical hock too fruity to go with savoury dishes. I am inclined to agree, and feel that perhaps such wines – along with the elegant semi-sweet whites of the Loire, say; the *amabili* whites of Italy (which are sweetish but not so fully so as the *dolci*); and the more down-to-earth rieslings of the Balkan countries – are best drunk by themselves, cool, as it might be on a summer's evening in the garden, after a light supper with a glass of rosé.

Drier wines come from other parts of Germany, and I am glad to see more often in this country nowadays the dry, full-flavoured *steinwein* of Franconia, in its flagon-shaped *bocksbeutel*, which is named after an unmentionable part of a billy-goat's anatomy, but a damn sight more pleasing to the eye.

I have lauded the width of range among white wines and find, still, that I have not mentioned how refreshing and appetizing is a glass of a cool, basically dry yet ever so slightly sweet, white wine as an eye-opener before a meal – or the wise old Frenchman who boasted that he was hale and hearty at eighty-seven because no water – no liquid other than wine – had ever passed his lips.

'How about cleaning your teeth?' enquired one young know-all.

'For that, monsieur, I use an unassuming, dry white wine ...'

Liz

While red wine can only be used to cook dishes in which the colour is an asset, white wine can be used in many more, particularly for cooking fish and poultry. And as white wine can be drunk with meat, there is something to be said for the German idea of drinking a rather sharp white wine with a rich dish, as this helps to cut the richness, while a more full-bodied red wine would make the meal heavy. I remember drinking a fresh crisp Mosel as an accompaniment to sucking pig – unexpected, but delicious.

Fish is often cooked in white wine (cider makes a good alternative), and here is a dish which is best made with sole.

SOLE IN WHITE WINE SAUCE

Make a fish stock by simmering the fish trimmings and bones with a chopped onion, parsley, salt, pepper, a glass of white wine and about a pint and a half of water. Simmer for half an hour, then strain the liquid into a bowl. Roll up eight fillets of sole, put them in a shallow pan and poach them very gently in some of the fish stock until they are just cooked. Meanwhile make the sauce by heating an ounce of butter in a saucepan, with the same amount of flour; let it cook for a few moments and then add the rest of the stock, stirring so that it is smooth, and simmering for ten minutes. Beat up two egg yolks with a tablespoon of cream, mix in a little of the hot liquid, and return the whole to the pan and mix well, but take care not to let it boil again.

Slice four ounces of mushrooms finely, cook them gently in a little butter, then put them over the bottom of a shallow serving dish. Put the drained cooked fillets on top of them, add some peeled cooked shrimps (mussels too, if you like), cover with the sauce and brown quickly under a hot grill.

Sole fillets, 8; mushrooms, 4oz; shrimps, ½ pint; egg yolks, 2; butter, 2oz; flour, 1oz; cream, 1 tablespoon. Fish stock

A less ambitious version of this rich and rather expensive dish can be made with cheaper fish, such as whiting fillets:

BAKED FILLETS IN WHITE WINE

Mix together four ounces of sliced mushrooms, two finely chopped shallots, a teaspoon of chives and a tablespoon of parsley. Spread half this mixture over the bottom of a well-buttered shallow baking dish, sprinkle with a thin layer of breadcrumbs, and add a pound and a half of white fish fillets. Cover with the remaining vegetable mixture, another layer of breadcrumbs and a tablespoon of grated cheese. Dot with butter, mix a glass of white wine with the same amount of water or fish stock, pour this over the fish and bake the dish in a moderate oven for half an hour.

Fish fillets, 1½lb; mushrooms, ¼lb; chives; parsley; shallots, 2; breadcrumbs, 2–3oz; grated cheese, 1oz; white wine, ¼ pint; water or stock, ¼ pint; butter

Herrings and mackerel are both rich, oily fishes, and one way to offset this is to souse them and eat them cold. Too many recipes for the souse consist almost entirely of vinegar, which makes the dish too sharp for many people, including me. However, an excellent souse can be made with only a little vinegar if it is mixed with white wine or cider.

SOUSED HERRINGS OR MACKEREL

Make the souse with half a pint of water, half a pint of white wine and a quarter of a pint of cider or white wine vinegar, two onions sliced into rings, two carrots also cut into thin rings, a bayleaf and a few peppercorns. Bring this to the boil and simmer for ten minutes or so while you prepare the fish, by cutting off the heads and removing the backbones and, of course, cleaning them if the fishmonger has not already done so. Let the souse cool slightly, add the fish, and simmer for about fifteen minutes. Let the fish cool in the liquor, and serve very cold. The fish look more appetizing if the skin is removed after they have cooled. Serve garnished with a few of the onion rings and carrots, and the souse poured over them.

Herrings or mackerel, 6; water, ½ pint; white wine, ½ pint; vinegar, ¼ pint; onions, 2; carrots, 2; bayleaf; peppercorns

Mackerel can be cooked in many of the ways associated with more expensive fish. This way, cooked with almonds, for instance, a way more usually associated with trout, goes well with a Loire white wine.

MACKEREL WITH ALMONDS

Clean and behead the fish but otherwise leave them whole, and prepare them by making two or three diagonal cuts along each side so that the heat penetrates more easily. For four fish, melt two ounces of butter in a frying pan and when it is hot cook the fish for ten minutes, turn them over, and cook the other side for the same time.

When they are cooked through, put them on to a hot dish and keep them warm. Brown two ounces of flaked almonds in the butter remaining in the pan, increasing the heat slightly to do so. Pour the buttery juices and almonds over the fish, and serve garnished with slices of lemon.

Mackerel, 4; butter, 2oz; almond flakes, 2oz

Trout itself is, of course, delicious if fresh (frozen trout tastes of nothing at all). A good way to cook it is in a Riesling, from Germany or Alsace, or a Vouvray from the Loire.

POACHED TROUT

Slice an onion and four carrots and add half a bottle of white wine – preferably a riesling or Vouvray – season with salt, peppercorns and thyme, and simmer for half an hour. This mixture is rather similar to the souse for the herring, without the vinegar, but this time the fish is eaten hot. When the liquid has cooked for half an hour, put in the whole fish and poach until done. Serve accompanied by freshly cooked carrots, and tiny onions if possible, and drink with them a glass of the wine they were poached in.

Trout, 4; onion, 1; carrots, 4; white wine, ½ bottle; peppercorns; salt; thyme

The white wines of Germany, Alsace, Yugoslavia and
northern Italy are particularly good for cooking, more so than
the heavier white burgundies or the sweeter Graves, though
these latter are sometimes needed for particular flavours. This
chicken dish cooked in riesling is much lighter than the better
known *coq au vin* and, because it is pale in colour, the same
wine can be drunk with it.

COQ AU RIESLING

Cut a roasting chicken into pieces and brown them in a
mixture of butter and oil. When they are well coloured, remove them from the pan while you soften in any remaining
fat a chopped onion and one or two carrots cut into thin
rings. Replace the chicken pieces, add a crushed tooth of
garlic, and season with salt and pepper. Warm a couple of
tablespoons of brandy, light the brandy and pour over the
chicken, shaking the pan until the flame dies down. Sprinkle
with flour and stir it in so that it browns a little, add thyme
and a bayleaf and then pour over the chicken half a bottle of
Riesling or similar light white wine. Leave to simmer
gently until the chicken is tender.

Remove the chicken pieces, and keep them warm on a
serving dish while you thicken the sauce with an egg yolk
beaten up in a tablespoon of cream. You can strain the sauce
of carrot and onion before thickening, or serve it with the
vegetables in, which I prefer. Pour the sauce over the chicken
and serve.

*Chicken, 1; onion, 1; carrots, 2; garlic; salt; pepper; thyme;
bayleaf; brandy, 2 tablespoons; flour; egg yolk, 1; cream, 1
tablespoon; white wine, ½ bottle; butter and oil*

Lamb is more usually cooked in red wine, but this is one way
of cooking it in white, and white wine is a good accompaniment too. Veal can be used the same way, of course, though it
is less easy to get good veal in Britain.

BLANQUETTE OF LAMB

Cut a pound and a half of lamb into one inch cubes, chop an
onion and two rashers of bacon quite small and brown all
slowly in lard or dripping. Season with salt and pepper,
sprinkle two tablespoons of flour over the meat, and stir well.
Add a glass of white wine, allowing it to bubble until it
reduces, then add water just to cover the meat and simmer
for about three-quarters of an hour or until the lamb is
tender. Add the juice of half a lemon and some chopped
parsley, beat two egg yolks in a bowl, pour in a little of the
hot liquid to mix, then return them to the saucepan, stirring
the liquid so that it thickens, but do not let it boil again.

*Lamb, 1½lb; onion, 1; bacon rashers, 2; lard, 1oz; flour, 2oz; salt;
pepper; white wine, 1 glass; water; egg yolks, 2; lemon juice;
parsley*

In Germany and Austria very much more white wine is
drunk than red and, as I've mentioned before, quite rich full-
flavoured dishes are accompanied by white wines. One dish,
called beef olives, *oiseaux sans têtes*, *loose-tinken* or beef roulades,
according to where you eat it, is made this way in Germany, and
accompanied by white wine.

ROULADE OF BEEF

This can be made big enough for one roulade to serve as a
portion, or made smaller, in which case allow three or four
pieces for each person. Cut some thin slices of buttock steak
into pieces about four inches square, and flatten them with a
meat bat. Spread each piece with mustard, then put on some
matchstick-sized pieces of onion, bacon and gherkin. Roll
the meat up with the stuffing inside and tie with string or
secure with cocktail sticks. Roll in flour then seal the outside
by frying quickly in dripping. Add sufficient stock or water
just to cover the meat rolls, cover the pan and cook gently
until the meat is tender – about half an hour. When cooked,
remove the meat from the pan and put on to a warm dish
while you add two or three tablespoons of sour cream to the

sauce (yogurt can be used instead); stir well then pour the
sauce over the meat and serve hot.

*Buttock steak, 1½lb; bacon rashers, 2; onion, 1; gherkin; stock or
water; sour cream, 2–3 tablespoons; mustard; flour; dripping*

Part of the wine-making process is to clarify or 'fine' the
young wine still in barrel by using beaten egg whites in much
the same way as stock is clarified – so in wine-growing regions
there are a lot of egg yolks to use up.

I have heard complaints in the claret country of the richness
of yolk-only omelettes, but custardy dishes are another answer, and here is a rich one made with the sweet wines of
Bordeaux. Like many dishes that have to be cooked slowly in
the oven it should be done in a *bain-marie*. This need be
nothing more than a large dish with water in it, into which the
custard dish is put, so that the cooking process is controlled,
rather on the principle of using a double saucepan. The classic
bain-marie is said to date from the fourth century, when a
Jewish alchemist named Mary devised a method of retaining
heat for the metals and vessels she was using for her experi-
ments. She used heated sand and kept the vessels in that, but the
modern version is rather simpler.

CRÈME BACCHIQUE
Bring to simmering point three quarters of a pint of sweet
white wine – ideally a sauternes or barsac, but other sweet
wine will do. Beat together four egg yolks and two ounces
of sugar until thick, and when the wine is hot pour slowly
into the egg mixture and stir well. Pour into individual
ramekins, and bake in a *bain-marie* in a moderate oven for
about forty minutes, or until the custard is set. Leave to get
quite cold before serving.

Sweet white wine, ¾ pint; egg yolks, 4; sugar, 2oz

This next dish, although it has a French name, is said to have
originated in Scotland, by way of Trinity College, Cambridge,

and is one of the most delicious of all custard dishes. The custard part can be made the day before it is needed if more convenient, leaving the top crust to be added later. Once the crisp top has been made don't put the custard into the re-frigerator or it may go soft – the whole point of this dish is the contrast between the crisp top and the soft underneath.

CRÈME BRÛLÉE

Bring half a pint of single cream (or half thick cream and half milk) nearly to boiling point. Beat together the yolks of three eggs and three ounces of sugar, then pour on to them the hot cream. Return this mixture to the heat and stir for a few minutes to thicken slightly, then pour the custard into one large, or preferably four small, ramekins. Bake in a *bain-marie* in a moderate oven until set, remove from the oven and let the custard get quite cold.

Pre-heat the grill, and when it is really hot sprinkle the tops of the custard with an even layer of granulated sugar. Put the dishes under the grill so that the sugar dissolves and browns – this is the tricky part of the whole operation as the grill must be hot enough for the sugar to melt without the underneath custard cooking any more. When this is done let the custard cool again, when the top should be smooth, brown, crisp, and wafer-thin.

Egg yolks, 3; caster sugar, 3oz; cream, $\frac{1}{2}$ pint; granulated sugar

There is all the difference in the world between the so-called 'custard' that is nothing more, in fact, than a thin sauce made of cornflour and colouring, bought in a packet, and true baked custards that are sweet and rich yet delicate.

This one calls for brandy, but rum or whisky or any other spirit can be used instead.

COQUE AU LAIT

Heat a pint of milk almost to boiling point. Heat together three ounces of sugar, the yolks of six eggs with the whites of three, and a tablespoon of thick cream. Beat until thick and

light, then pour the hot milk slowly into the mixture,
stirring all the time. Add a tablespoon of brandy or other
spirit, pour the whole into a well buttered baking dish and
cook in a slow oven (300° gas 2) until the custard is set,
which will be in about half an hour. Serve well chilled,
either by itself or with baked apples.

*Milk, 1 pint; egg yolks, 6; egg whites, 3; cream, 1 tablespoon;
sugar, 3oz*

(Whites of egg left over from any of these recipes will
keep in the refrigerator, covered, and can be used for the
macaroons mentioned in chapter 2, or for meringues.)

Fruit dishes are sometimes too acid to go well with wine, but
the following dishes are good with a sweet white wine.

BUTTERED PEACHES
Allow a peach and a half for each person. Skin some slightly
under-ripe peaches (this is best done by pouring boiling
water over them, and letting them stand for a few moments,
when the skin should come off quite easily). Slice them as
neatly as possible and arrange the slices in a shallow dish,
cover them with a layer of soft brown sugar and dot gener-
ously with butter. Put them under a hot grill just long
enough for the slices to soften a little and for the sugar and
butter to melt together into a delicious sauce. Serve warm.

Peaches, 6; butter, 1½oz; brown sugar, 2oz

STUFFED PEACHES
Skin five ripe peaches and cut four of them in half, remove
the stones and scoop out a little of the surrounding flesh to
make the hollows bigger. Keep this to add to the fifth peach
which should have the stone removed and the flesh mashed
to a pulp. To this mashed peach add a tablespoon of sugar,
an ounce and a half of butter, the yolk of an egg and two
ounces of crumbled macaroons or ratafias. Fill each peach

half with this mixture, put the fruit into a shallow dish and cook, uncovered, in a moderate oven for about half an hour. Serve hot or cold.

Peaches, 5; sugar, 1 tablespoon; butter, 1½oz; egg yolk, 1; macaroons or ratafias, 2oz

BOODLE'S FOOL

This originated at Boodle's Club and is still regularly on the menu there. Similar to a syllabub but, as it is made with oranges, it is less rich.

Line a bowl with pieces of sponge cake cut into slices about half an inch thick. Grate the rinds of two oranges and one lemon, squeeze the juice from the fruit and mix rind, juice and a tablespoon of sugar together.

In another bowl whip half a pint of cream until it is thickened but not stiff, then slowly add the juice to this, continuing to beat so that the orange mixture is incorporated into the cream and the cream will get thicker. Pour all this over the sponge cakes so that they are completely covered and chill thoroughly for at least two hours so that the juice can penetrate into the sponge, and the cream firm up a little.

Oranges, 2; lemon, 1; sugar, 1 tablespoon; double cream, ½ pint; sponge cake

CREAMY APPLES

This can either be made in a fireproof dish or you can make a flan case, baked blind, and put the apples on that. I prefer it in the dish as the pastry makes the whole dish rather solid.

Mix together four ounces of sugar with an ounce of flour, a pinch of salt and one of cinnamon. The sugar can be brown or white, but brown has more flavour. Peel, core and slice thinly and evenly a pound of apples and drop the slices into the sugar and flour. Toss the apples in this mixture so that they are coated with it, then arrange the slices neatly in the dish, or on the flan case. Sprinkle on any remaining sugar and flour, then pour a quarter pint of cream over the fruit.

Bake in a moderately hot oven for about forty minutes, until the apples are soft and beginning to brown a little. Serve hot or cold, but it is at its best when just warm.

Apples, 1lb; sugar, 4oz; flour, 1oz; cinnamon; salt; cream, ¼ pint

CHAPTER FOUR

In the Pink

ONE occasion when I fell under the gaze of *Private Eye*, I found myself pilloried in the Pseuds' Corner of that frolicsome fortnightly for having observed in a newspaper article that what I liked with a simple summer-time picnic luncheon was 'wine of an engaging pink . . . wine that looks pretty and need not be taken too damned seriously: a sort of popsy of a wine.'

I did not feel then, nor do I feel now, that there is anything particularly pseudish about expressing a preference for popsies and pinkers, and I shall maintain until I have lost all interest in either that these are what is proper for a picnic.

Or for a summertime supper come to that or, especially, a buffet luncheon, which to my mind ought to be a sort of indoor picnic, at which noble burgundies or high-and-mighty hocks would be overdoing it: you cannot drink a serious wine standing up. Rosé is the wine that one chooses for lightness in the mouth and pleasure to the eye.

This latter is why I would always choose to have it served decanted into clear, colourless glass jugs or carafes or, better still, for I like pink wine to be served cool (but never, never,

never diluted by ice melting into the glass or the carafe), in one of those Italian wicker-covered *fiaschi* that have a separate compartment for ice, or in one of those German silver-mounted jugs with a detachable ice-cylinder.

I have an especial affection for pink champagne, but as an aperitif – I do not care for fizz with food. The champenois themselves do, though, and serve old, dry champagnes with fruit and sweet puddings, a combination I do not care for at all.

The various Portuguese *vinhos verdes*, which are not green in colour, but in age, and may be either white or pink, are only semi-sparkling and have a touch of sweetness – as does their near-relative, the ubiquitous Mateus Rosé. These make pleasant enough aperitif wines, too, but the heavily advertised are highly priced . . .

Three years running, each year on Midsummer's Eve, the house of Mentzendorff, which ships the pink Provençal wines of Maison Ott, and that of Moët and Chandon, responsible for more than one fine brand of pink champagne, put on, at my prompting, a 'La Vie en Rose' dinner.

Everything was pink – the men's ties or shirts or button-holes; the women's dresses or ribbons or sprays of flowers; the table linen and the bowls of carnations and – to take one dinner as an example – the iced beetroot soup and the mousse of York ham, the salmon and the strawberries and cream.

It was the sort of dinner at which a great white burgundy or some fine Alsatian or German wine might well normally have been served with the main course; and there are friends of mine in the wine trade, and much respected colleagues of mine who write about wine who feel strongly that no important dinner party is complete without a wine or wines of that sort – wines to be taken seriously.

My view, though, is that just as there is a place in the theatre for *The Importance of Being Earnest* and for Restoration comedy as well as for *King Lear*, just as there is a place for Offenbach and Lehár as well as for Verdi and Wagner, so there is a place at table for wines that are pleasing to the eye and easy to drink, as well as for great wines that are to be subjects for learned discussion.

A summer-evening supper party is meant to be light-hearted, and I know of no better way to begin it than with pink champagne. I remember one such party in my own house, when my then octogenarian mother-in-law, handed her glass on arrival, held it up to the light and exclaimed, 'Pink champagne! How *very* pretty!' and a girl at her heels, a quarter her age, holding up *her* glass, saying 'Pink champagne! What *fun*!'

There is a lot to be said for prettiness and for fun: I cannot think of better reasons for serving or for drinking a wine.

It is permitted, and it is usual, to make pink champagne by adding a little of the still red wine of the region at a particular stage in the making of what would otherwise be a wine of the classic gold, but still rosés are made by running the juice of black grapes off the skins after a longer time than a white wine would have (all – or virtually all – grape juice is colourless, and some white wines, champagne among them, are made from black grapes) but, unlike reds, before fermentation.

This means that not only does the wine derive less colour than a red wine would, but less body, flavour and staying power, from pips and skins, which is why pink wine should be light and fresh in the mouth, and why I like to drink it young and cool.

What it does not mean is that pink wines are necessarily less heady.

Alcohol comes not from pips and skins but from the sugar in the juice, and many white and pink wines are alcoholically as strong as, or stronger than, the fullest-flavoured and deepest-coloured reds.

Many a carefully nurtured young English miss has holidayed in Spain or in Italy, unaware of this elementary truth, and many a wicked Latin, twirling his moustache, has taken advantage of the fact – and of the carefully nurtured young English miss.

Tavel rosé, for instance, from the Châteauneuf du Pape region, perhaps the most important of all French – indeed, of any – pink wines, hailed by one great authority, Morton Shand, as, 'beautifully clean to the palate, in colour a joy to the eye, dry and yet *fruité*, it has just the right degree of flavour and vinosity', has been condemned by the equally distinguished Edward Hyams as 'quarrelsome'.

Which can, of course, be said of any wine drunk perhaps too eagerly and perhaps under a hot sun, as many picnic wines are.

Both bigwigs were right: what makes Tavel more reliable in quality than many wines shipped here is that it 'travels' well, and what makes it travel well is a relatively high alcoholic content for a light table wine. This is also why Tavel is the only rosé to keep well. But these very qualities, of reliability and staying power, derive from those that make it more suitable for dull days indoors than for sun-baked luncheons *al fresco*, for which I prefer lighter, less distinguished, pinks from countries other than France, or from the Midi, or – prettiest of all, perhaps – from the Loire valley, where some of the pink Anjou and Saumur wines, made from the same grapes as the finest clarets, have a light, fresh fragrance and an enchanting whisper of fruit.

But, then, all taste in wine is highly subjective, which is why, no doubt, the rosé I have always enjoyed most, whenever it comes my way, is not the aristocratic Tavel, with its true, clear, colour, nor one of the charmers from the Loire, but one of those cheaper, less good-looking, no doubt less nice-tasting, *pelure d'oignon* wines from the Midi, so-called because their colour is the thin translucent tawny of onion-skin, and not a true pink.

And all because one of them is the wine of the house at a little *bistro* in Paris that I have been going to since the Liberation, when a bottle was planted firmly on the table, with the compliments of the *patron*, because I was in British uniform, and I tasted it for the first time.

A wine, therefore, that for all sorts of nostalgic reasons, because it brings back those days when all the men I knew were brave, and all the girls were pretty – or so it seems to me now – I have drunk at every meal I have had there in the thirty years since, with beef bourguignon, with roast chicken, with kidneys in red wine, and with who knows what.

There is plenty of pink wine about, much of it as delicious to drink as it is pretty to look at, but it is worth while choosing

with care, for some can be thin and mawkish – merely pink and sweetish, and with nothing else to say for itself.

Rather like the one served in a small London restaurant to a friend of mine, on leave from abroad, who complained to the waitress that it not only looked, but also tasted, like inferior port, watered down.

'Oh, no sir', replied the waitress: 'I don't think there could be any mistake of *that* sort. We don't make it ourselves, you know: we buy it already bottled, from Rosé.'

A former colleague of mine – Aidan Philip, now dead, who used to write quirkily erudite cookery articles in *The Observer* under the name 'Syllabub' – once devised a menu for a young woman, anxious to precipitate a proposal, to prepare for her intended victim.

Mulligatawny soup, he suggested; trout in aspic, new potatoes and salad, strawberry-orange fool and one good cheese, adding that 'a good but safe wine is advisable. A *vin rosé* meets the case, but it should be a Tavel or a very dry one from Provence'.

This is not the way I was myself brought up to scratch, and I am no judge in these matters. I think, though, that pink Provençal wines are too dry for the matter in hand, and I am not sure that Tavel is quite the right choice in the circumstances, save that, as I have already indicated, it is stronger than it looks, which may be what is needed . . .

After all, given the right frame of mind, anything will do. When Dick Swiveller bade Little Nell's brother 'fan the sinking flame of hilarity with the wing of friendship; pass the rosy', the rosy was a jug of cold gin and water.

Liz

Picnics and buffet luncheons are what the Master thinks of as the occasions for rosé, so here is a recipe that does very well for either – one of the family's favourite picnic dishes – a minced-meat tart, which is as easy to eat in the fingers as a ham sandwich and a good deal more moist and tasty:

PICNIC TART
Make a short-crust pastry with eight ounces of flour, and four ounces of mixed butter and lard, with cold water to mix.

Chop a medium onion finely and soften it in butter, but take care that it does not brown. Add three-quarters of a pound of raw minced beef and turn it in the onion and butter until it loses its redness. Add a little chopped mushroom or kidney and sprinkle with flour. Cook for a few minutes, adding a little stock or water, just to moisten, but the mixture should not be too soft. Season well with salt, pepper and Worcester sauce. Let this cool while half the pastry is used to line a flan tin. Fill the flan to the brim with the meat mixture, brush the edge of the pastry with beaten egg, cover with the rest of the pastry as a lid, make one or two diagonal slits in the top, brush with egg and bake in a moderately hot oven (400° gas 6) for half an hour. Leave to get quite cold before cutting.

Short-crust pastry, 8oz; minced beef, $\frac{3}{4}$lb; onion, 1; kidney or mushroom, $\frac{1}{4}$lb; flour; salt; pepper; Worcester sauce; beaten egg, 1; butter; stock or water

This recipe for a salmon and prawn pâté is more expensive, but rich, and the amounts given should be sufficient for eight people, or half quantities can be used quite successfully. Although I dislike chilled salmon by itself, it serves quite well for a made-up dish like this.

SALMON AND PRAWN PÂTÉ

Sauté a finely chopped onion and a tooth of garlic in a little butter, together with a bayleaf and chopped parsley. Add half a pound of salmon and half a pound of white fish – coley or whiting if you are feeling economical, turbot or halibut if you prefer – then pour in a glass of rosé. Mix well and cook until the liquid is almost absorbed. Add a glass of water or fish stock and cook for ten minutes, or until the fish is cooked. Remove the fish from the pan, and reduce the liquid by half by boiling rapidly.

Remove all the skin and bones from the fish, put through the mincer with half a pound of cooked prawns. Season with salt and pepper and half a glass of brandy. Dissolve half an ounce of gelatine in the cooled fish liquid, add half a pint of cream and beat the whole well together until the mixture is smooth. Put into a serving dish and let it set in the refrigerator.

Salmon, ½lb; white fish, ½lb; prawns, ½lb; rosé, 1 glass; cream, ½ pint; onion, 1; bayleaf; garlic; salt; pepper; brandy; parsley; gelatine; water or fish stock

Another fishy dish that might have done for one of the pink dinners that Ray mentions:

PRAWN SOUP

Shell half a pound of prawns, put the fish aside in a bowl, rinse the shells in a colander and put them into a saucepan with two pints of water, or so that they are well covered. Simmer the shells in a covered pan for about half an hour when the liquid will have reduced considerably.

Chop an onion finely, cook in a little butter until it is transparent. Chop the prawns roughly, add them to the onion, and pour in the strained liquid from the shells. Simmer until the onion is quite soft, put the soup into the blender until smooth. Taste for seasoning, as sometimes the prawns can be very salty. Just before serving, add two or three tablespoons of cream and serve hot. Whole prawns can be added for garnish.

Prawns, ½lb; water, 2 pints; onion, butter, ½oz; cream, 2–3 tablespoons

Rosé is not often thought of as a cooking wine, but here is a chicken recipe that uses it; is good hot or cold; and is a much lighter and more summery dish than the more conventional *coq au vin* made with red wine.

CHICKEN IN ROSÉ

Joint a roasting chicken and roll the pieces in well-seasoned flour. Heat a mixture of butter and oil in a shallow pan, add the chicken and cook until they are browned. When well coloured remove from the pan and put into a casserole. In the same pan, adding more oil and butter if needed, cook half a pound of mushrooms, then add them to the chicken in the casserole.

Pour a quarter-pint of chicken stock into the pan, stir well so that it mixes with the juices left there, then pour over the chicken and mushroom. Add half a pint of rosé, add a sprig of fresh tarragon (or half a teaspoon of dried), season with salt and pepper, cover the casserole and cook in a moderate oven for about three-quarters of an hour, adding a little more wine during the cooking if necessary. Uncover the casserole, turn the oven down to 300° gas 2, and continue cooking until the chicken is quite tender.

Chicken, 1; mushrooms, ½lb; chicken stock, ¼ pint; rosé wine, ¾ pint; tarragon; butter; oil; salt; pepper; flour

Now here is a dish that I first came across in Champagne, served at the Château de Saran, that splendid house at which the hospitable firm of Moët and Chandon entertain their guests. It is a pretty dish to go with a pretty wine – in this case a sweet rosé – and as it is decorated with rose petals this is the place for it.

PECHES EUGÉNIE

Peel some ripe peaches, put them in a dish with strawberries and sprinkle a little sugar and maraschino over them.
Leave them in a cold place for an hour or so.

Make a sabayon sauce: beat four egg yolks with three
ounces of sugar, and whisk over a low flame. Gradually add
a quarter of a bottle of champagne and thicken by whisking
the mixture in the top part of a double boiler. Continue to
beat until thick, then remove from the heat and beat again
over ice until the mixture is quite cold.

Put the peaches and strawberries on to a large oval platter,
pour on the sauce just before serving them and decorate
with a red rose in the centre, and alternate red and yellow
rose petals round the edge of the dish.

*Peaches; strawberries; marschino; egg yolks, 4; sugar, 3–4oz;
champagne, $\frac{1}{4}$ bottle*

Another summery fruit dish that would go with one of the
fruitier rosés is strawberry tart.

STRAWBERRY TART

Make a pastry with five ounces of plain flour, three ounces of
softened butter, two ounces of caster sugar, and bind with an
egg yolk. When the mixture is made, leave it to rest in a
cool place for half an hour. Roll out and put into a fluted
flan ring or tin, trim the edges, prick the bottom of the
pastry with a fork, then bake for fifteen minutes at 350° gas
4 until light brown. (It is advisable to cover the bottom of the
pastry with foil on which a few beans are scattered, which
will stop the middle of the pastry rising up.) When the
pastry is cooked, remove from the oven and cool.

Prepare three quarters of a pound of strawberries by removing the stalks. Mix four ounces of cream cheese with
two tablespoons of single cream and spread over the base of
the flan. Cover this with the strawberries arranged pointing

upwards, sitting on their stalk ends. Melt three tablespoons of red currant jelly, then pour over the strawberries and leave to set.

Pastry: *flour, 5oz; butter, 3oz; egg yolk, 1; caster sugar, 2oz*
Filling: *cream cheese, 4oz; single cream, 2 tablespoons; straw-berries, ¾lb; red currant jelly, 3 tablespoons*

And finally a pink cheese:

LIPTAUER
Mash a quarter of a pound of curd cheese (or, if you use cottage cheese, sieve it first) with a little butter, then add a heaped teaspoon of sweet paprika, or enough to give a pleasing colour to the cheese, half a teaspoon of caraway seeds, a teaspoon of chopped capers, a teaspoon of chopped gherkins, a sprinkling of salt and garlic salt. Mix well together and heap on to a dish. Eat with plain biscuits or rye bread.

Curd cheese, ¼lb; butter, ½oz; paprika, 1 teaspoon; capers, 1 teaspoon; gherkins, 1 teaspoon; caraway seeds, ½ teaspoon; salt; garlic salt

CHAPTER FIVE

A Few Words about Fizz

'I SHOULD here, perhaps, acknowledge the consolation I have never failed to find in the fermented juice of the grape. Writing in my sixty-fourth year, I can truthfully say that since I reached the age of discretion I have consistently drunk more than most people would say was good for me. Nor do I regret it. Wine has been to me a firm friend and a wise counsellor.'

Most wine-lovers have been reminded, on this or on that occasion, of Duff Cooper's tribute to wine in his autobiography, *Old Men Forget*. What prompted it was the elderly author's recollection of an imperial pint of Veuve Clicquot he had consumed forty years earlier, a bored and lonely private soldier on leave from a Guards training battalion, in the echoing emptinesses of a blacked-out Royal Automobile Club on a wet Sunday evening.

The significance is in the bubble.

Champagne is not noticeably stronger in alcohol than a still table wine – claret, say, or a white burgundy – but people who know about this kind of thing tell me that its bubble carries alcohol's tonic effect more quickly into the bloodstream than a still wine can.

Its exhilarating effect, therefore, is immediate. Hence Hilaire Belloc's rather back-handed compliment – that he only drank champagne 'to raise me up from the dead', to which he thoughtfully added, 'a thing I constantly need'.

This, though, seems to me the least worthy of the many reasons for drinking champagne. The lightness of body, the delicacy of flavour, and the elegance of style – the very prettiness of the bubbles steadily rising through the pale golden liquid – make it the most appetizing of appetizers, the most festive of festive drinks. John Jorrocks was nearer to it than Belloc with his 'it gives one werry gentlemanly ideas', and we have all experienced Mr Alan Brien's sensation, on drinking champagne, 'of being given a physical lift, like water wings'.

It is these qualities that make champagne, to me, the best of all pre-prandial appetizers, or mid-morning pick-me-ups, and my father-in-law used to tell of a man at his generally rather hearty Oxford college, at the turn of the century, who announced, on more than one hungover morning, that 'it was simply sickening: I'd no appetite at *all* for breakfast, so I sent out for a bottle of fizz and a dressed crab'.

(It is unfair to the reputation of my reverend father-in-law as a raconteur and a mimic not to add that his frail friend lisped . . .)

I do not myself, as a rule, drink champagne with grub, though the people who make it do, and many a good book by better-informed wine-lovers than I am pronounces it the one wine that can be drunk throughout any meal.

It can, but I don't. . . .

But just as I count it the prince of appetizers, so do I love it dearly in combination: the light and light-hearted Buck's Fizz, which consists of two parts of champagne to one of freshly squeezed fresh orange-juice, served very cold in a tall glass, is a delicious warm-weather drink, and Black Velvet – Guinness and champagne, half-and-half – is as heartening a pick-me-up on a winter's morning.

There are, literally, hundreds of brands of champagne – at least a score, well known in this country, all of which are particularly good, differing between themselves not in quality but

in style, this one drier, that one fruitier, another one lighter, so
that choosing between them is a matter of personal taste: Winston Churchill was devoted to Pol Roger, Nubar Gulbenkian to Krug, André Simon to Pommery.

As I have written a whole book about it, it would be idle to conceal that I am especially fond, myself, of Bollinger.

But there *are* sparkling wines from other parts of France, made in the same way. They are not so expensive, for they lack the prestige of champagne and usually, it must be admitted, some of the finesse. But there are nevertheless some uncommonly good wines among them. So if it is bubbles you are after, let us look for wines that are cheaper than champers.

If good grapes from classic wine-growing areas are used, then the *méthode champenoise* will ensure a sparkling wine of real distinction. Among the best I know, save for champagne itself, is the sparkler of Seyssel, which is in the upper valley of the Rhône, not far from the Swiss frontier, and with a view of Mont Blanc. I drink a lot of it at home, for it is two-thirds the price of the cheapest champagne. I have never tried to pass it off as champagne, but more than one knowledgeable guest, offered a glass as an apéritif, has mistaken it for such until I enlightened him.

Similar wines are made in the same way in the Loire: Hilaire Belloc, an opinionated wine-lover, actually rated those of Vouvray and Saumur higher than champagne itself. That was dotty of him, but he disliked very dry wines and appreciated their slightly greater fruit. Certainly they are delicious and excellent value.

Fruitier still, though undoubtedly dry, are the best of the German sparkling wines – those, whether from the Rhine or the Mosel, that are made wholly or largely from the classic riesling grape. The cheaper German sparklers are pleasant enough to drink, but lack the fragrance and fruitiness of the more expensive wines. The sparkling Mosels tend to be the drier and lighter, the hocks (Rhine wines) rather bigger-bodied.

From Burgundy come both red and white sparkling wines, but the best burgundian bubbles are to be found in the bottles that contain a pink wine, expressively named *oeil de perdrix* – partridge-eye. There is not a great deal about, but it is worth looking for, being crisp and delicate to the taste and prettily pleasing to the eye. As I said of pink champagne in a previous chapter, it puts one's guests in a summery frame of mind.

All the wines I have mentioned so far are dry or dryish, but the best-known of all sparkling wines other than champagne is not at all dry. The Italian Asti Spumante is a sparkling white made from the muscat grape, and is strongly aromatic of that delicious fruit. Sweet though it is, the bubbles and the delicacy of the wine itself prevent it from being rich or cloying.

It is delicious after dinner, with fresh fruit, at a young people's party, or at a summer picnic, served very cool.

I recall that during the campaign in Italy, more than thirty years ago, I used to share a morning bottle with two other war correspondents. The bubbles gave us the courage to get to within binocular-range of the back areas of battle, and the sugar content the energy to get briskly back to our type-writers. How true it is to talk of the bubble reputation even in the cannon's mouth . . .

There are sophisticated, or would-be sophisticated, wine-drinkers who affect to look down on Asti because of its sweet-ness. This is to mistake the nature of the wine which the French (for all that they make, themselves, the greatest sparkling wine in the world) are much too wise to do. France has always been Italy's best foreign customer for Asti Spumante: Proust's Swann sent a case of it to Aunt Céline and Aunt Flora.

Indeed, she makes sweet, sparkling muscatel wines of her own, of which I suppose the best-known is the one made in the Saumur region of the Loire and sold under the brand-name 'Golden Guinea'.

I used to like it on the rare occasions that it came my way when I was a boy; then I became too sophisticated for so simple a pleasure, and used to turn up my nose at all sweet wines, especially sweet sparklers.

Now I am wise again, and know very well how good it is with a ripe peach or nectarine after dinner, or with a biscuit in the garden on a Sunday morning.

74

Liz

Champagne is never cheap, even in its native land, and it may seem extravagant to use it lavishly in cooking. Sometimes, though, only a little is needed, and sometimes, too, there may be a little left over in a bottle. Once in a way, for that matter, one may feel like being lavish, or any of the other dry sparkling wines mentioned may be used instead.

SOLE AU CHAMPAGNE

Clean and cut off the heads of four soles, and remove the skin from both sides. Put the cleaned fish into a buttered pan, cover with dry champagne, season with salt and pepper and poach gently until the fish are done.

Meanwhile beat three egg yolks and six ounces of cream together over hot water until the mixture thickens. Finish this sauce with one or two tablespoons of the liquid in which the fish were cooked.

Remove the soles from the pan, trim them of the small bones, place on a serving dish and pour the sauce over. Serve with plain boiled potatoes.

The small 'slip' soles will do very well for this dish, but not lemon sole – a different fish altogether.

Sole, 4; champagne, $\frac{1}{4}$ bottle; egg yolks, 3; cream, 6oz; butter; salt; pepper

Scallops are so delicious in themselves that they need very little in the way of additions; indeed, too much sauce or seasoning destroys their delicate flavour rather than enhancing or adding to it. This way, though, using a modest glass of champagne only, is an excellent way of preparing them.

SCALLOPS IN CHAMPAGNE

Allow two or three scallops per person, according to size. Wash them well, slice the white part into two or three, and season them lightly.

Melt two ounces of butter in a frying pan, put in an ounce of fresh white breadcrumbs, add a glass of champagne and the scallops and cook gently for five minutes or so. Remove the scallops from the pan and put them in their own deep shells, or in a fire-proof dish. Cover with fine toasted breadcrumbs and dot with butter. Bake in a moderate oven for about fifteen minutes.

Scallops, 8–12; butter, 5oz; fresh white breadcrumbs, 1oz; champagne, 1 glass; toasted breadcrumbs; salt; pepper

Elsewhere in this book I have given a recipe from the Château de Saran, where the hospitable house of Moët and Chandon entertains its friends so lavishly. Here is another, not a dish cooked with champagne, but white port (and called after another French district, the Charente, and I don't know why), but as I have eaten it only in Champagne, and it is good, it seems appropriate to give it here.

RIS DE VEAU CHARENTAISE
Soak the sweetbreads in water for two or three hours, then place in a pan of cold water and bring gently to the boil. Boil for a couple of minutes, then drain and plunge the sweetbreads into cold water. Let them cool between two plates so that they become slightly flattened, and easier to slice. Melt an ounce of butter, slice the sweetbreads and colour them in the butter, then remove and keep them warm. In the same pan cook some shallots or an onion, with a quarter pound of mushrooms sliced thinly. Add more butter as necessary. Mix into this two glasses of white port, then thicken with cream and season with salt and pepper. Cover the sweetbreads with this sauce and serve hot.

Sweetbreads, 1½lb; butter, 2oz; shallots or onion; mushrooms, ¼lb; white port, 2 glasses; salt; pepper ; cream

Many of the great champagne houses, including Moët, have their being in Epernay, where there is a charming hotel called the Berceaux, so-called because of the vaults in which the wine is kept, which are known as *berceaux*, or cradles. One of its many excellent dishes is this chicken in champagne.

POULET BERCEAUX

Cut a chicken in quarters, season and cook gently in butter in a casserole, but without letting the meat colour. When almost cooked flambé with a small glass of brandy, then deglaze the pan with half a bottle of champagne. Let the liquid reduce by about half then add half a pint of cream. Reduce again and add a dessertspoonful of tomato purée. Put the chicken pieces on to a serving dish, cover with the sauce and serve with rice.

Chicken, 1; butter; brandy, small glass; champagne, ½ bottle; cream, ½ pint; tomato purée, 1 dessertspoon

There is a champagne salad that is almost a meal in itself:

CHAMPENOISE SALAD

Cook two pounds of potatoes in their skins, let them cool, then skin and slice them finely. Top, tail and de-string a pound of green beans and boil them in salted water, then drain and cool. Hard boil four eggs. Put layers of the salad ingredients into a bowl thus: potatoes, beans, potatoes, sliced eggs, potatoes, anchovy fillets, potatoes, stoned olives, potatoes. Pour half a bottle of champagne over this mixture and leave for a couple of hours. Just before serving add a small glass of brandy and season with a mixture of olive oil, mustard, lemon juice, salt and pepper. Enough for six.

Potatoes, 2lb; eggs, 4; green beans, 1lb; anchovy fillets, small tin; olives, mixed black and green to taste; champagne, ½ bottle; lemon, 1; mustard; olive oil; salt; pepper; brandy, small glass

A useful sauce made with champagne is served with roast chicken or other birds, or with fish, which is sometimes cooked in it as well.

SAUCE RAVIGOTE

Pour a quarter bottle of champagne into a pan with two tablespoons of oil and the same of stock. Bring to the boil and reduce until there is little more than a glassful left. Add finely chopped parsley, chives and shallots with tarragon too if you like, and season with salt and pepper. Bring to the boil again and reduce further until it is a thickish sauce. Add some lemon juice before serving.

Champagne, ¼ bottle; oil, 2 tablespoons; stock (fish or chicken according to the dish it is to accompany), 2 tablespoons; parsley; chives; shallots; tarragon; salt; pepper; lemon juice

Wine is not Champagne's only gastronomic product: mustard from Meaux is almost as well-known. These mustards are flavoured with herbs and spices and are piquant rather than merely hot. The excellent Moutarde Florida comes from Magenta, a small suburb of Epernay, and is to be found in most of the shops of the little town in pots resembling champagne bottles.

I am told that this mustard is made with the wine lost from the bottles in the disgorgement process. One way to use these spicy French mustards is to mix them with butter, preferably unsalted, and to spread them over steaks or chops before grilling. Pork chops benefit particularly from this treatment. Allow about a tablespoon and a half to each quarter pound of butter, mix well together and keep in the refrigerator until wanted.

Some excellent cheeses, too, come from in or near Champagne. Probably the best known is Brie which, like the mustard, comes from near Meaux. This is one of the best of the French cheeses, and in good condition can hardly be surpassed. Others are Boursin, Boursault – very rich and creamy – Chaource, Coulommiers, and the rather strong-smelling cheeses such as Maroilles.

One way to serve Brie, particularly for one that is slightly under-ripe, is to cream it with white wine.

CRÈME DE BRIE

Take some Brie, scrape off the skin carefully, cover with dry white wine and let it stand overnight. Next day drain it, wipe it dry and cream with an ounce or so of unsalted butter, shape it into a round, coat it with very fine toasted crumbs, and put in the refrigerator for an hour or so until ready to serve.

Brie; butter; dry white wine; toasted crumbs

Pink champagne is one of the prettiest drinks I know – and it tastes as delicious as it looks. So this luxurious sorbet is for special occasions. It can be made with ordinary champagne, but would lose something of its looks.

PINK CHAMPAGNE SORBET

Combine seven ounces of sugar with the juice of half a lemon, just under half a pint of water and a quarter bottle of pink champagne. Stir the mixture to dissolve the sugar, strain into a mould and put into the freezing compartment of the refrigerator. Look at the mixture from time to time and scoop the crystals that form at the edge towards the middle of the bowl where the freezing is slower. When it is ready it should be slightly mushy and granular. Serve heaped in glasses, and just before serving sprinkle each glass with a spoonful of the champagne. If you are using an ice cream maker or sorbetière, there is no need to stir it as the machine will do it for you.

Sugar, 7oz; water, just under $\frac{1}{2}$ pint; lemon, $\frac{1}{2}$; pink champagne, $\frac{1}{4}$ bottle

Sometimes champagne is too dry to drink happily with the sweet course, but as part of the preparation of that course it is splendid. One of the simplest and most delicious desserts is champagne with peaches. For this, use one of the fruitier champagnes, or Asti if you want the muscatel flavour.

PEACHES IN CHAMPAGNE

Dip the peaches in boiling water then into cold so that their skins can be removed easily. Cut them into slices, put them in a bowl and add two or three tablespoons of sugar, according to the ripeness of the fruit. Pour over them a quarter bottle of champagne and leave in a cold place for at least two hours before serving chilled.

Peaches, 4; sugar, 2–3oz; champagne, $\frac{1}{4}$ bottle

Bad Companions

WHAT is the nastiest dish or drink you can possibly invent or imagine?

The poser was set as a daft, after-dinner competition one ribald evening, and the easy winner – streets ahead of concoctions so imaginatively vile that they could not be written even on a lavatory wall – was the simplest: a soup-plate of warm gin with a red hair in it.

When I recounted this to Nick Clarke, the larger-than-life character who runs Nick's Diner in darkest Fulham, he said that he had beaten a fellow-restaurateur in a similar contest with his creation: tram-driver's glove *en croûte*, in Brylcreem sauce.

I can think of nothing so nasty as either of these, but I still remember the British tycoon I met on holiday at a French hotel, who drank Mouton-Rothschild 1953 at every lunch and dinner ('very reliable people, the Rothschilds, o'boy'), washing it down each time with a tin of Coca-Cola, because red wine makes you so thirsty, o'boy.

And Wynford Vaughan-Thomas tells the story of the *vin d'honneur* given by the HQ staff of General Patch's United

States Seventh Army during the liberation of Burgundy to General de Montsabert and other distinguished French comrades-in-arms.

It was held, Wynford recounts, in an eighteenth-century palace in Besançon: 'trumpets sounded, and a column of waiters marched in, bearing bottles on silver trays. My heart gave a warning thump – the bottles were from Burgundy, the noblest gifts of the Côte and, horror of horrors, they were bubbling gently ...'

'We're in luck,' whispered a United States colonel in Wynford's ear. 'The doc' knows all about this Frog liquor: he's hotted it up with surgical spirit ...'

On more normal levels of experience, there are foods and wines that – to my fancy, at any rate – go ill together.

Dry red wines are good with cheese but not with fruit or with puddings, which is why the French serve the cheese before the chocolate mousse (and I wish that those who give public dinners in this country would do the same), so that one can carry on with the claret or burgundy of the main course before going on to a sauternes or a sweet champagne.

More particularly, not dishes so much as flavourings and relishes can kill a wine.

I am fond of cold roast beef.

I am fond of horseradish sauce with it (by which I do not mean a bottled sauce of – I quote a famous label – 'horseradish, vinegar, sugar, vegetable oil, cream, salt, skim-milk powder, acetic acid, egg, edible gum, mustard, emulsifier, colour, tartaric acid, lactic acid and flavourings', but real horseradish and real cream, or even horseradish simply grated over the beef in flakes).

I am fond of claret with cold roast beef.

But I am *not* fond of claret and horseradish sauce: one cannot taste the claret.

So I either have horseradish with my beef and drink beer (Carlsberg lager or Guinness) or the very cheapest carafe red on the restaurant's wine-list, and not much of it or, if I have my eye on a good claret, then I forego the horseradish. A little mild mustard is kinder.

The same is true of roast saddle of lamb, claret and mint sauce – mint sauce made with vinegar, that is: Liz has a way, shortly to be revealed, of flavouring the gravy with mint, a way that is benign beyond belief.

> *Malt does more than Milton can*
> *To justify God's ways to man –*

– but not malt vinegar which, when the British First Republic is proclaimed, and I am Commissar for Food and Drink, will be declared illegal, but not on pain of death, only of life imprisonment. The death penalty is to be reserved for those guilty of Non-Brewed Condiment, which I understand to be acetic acid coloured with caramel. I am, and always have been, opposed to capital punishment, but . . .

Liz makes her salad dressing with her own tarragon wine-vinegar; and at the Café Royal Grill Room, which is my favourite London eating-house, my friends Carlo and Vincenzo and John and Gino know how to make a lemon-and-oil dressing that seems to me not to quarrel with the Bordeaux red or the Loire white that I usually take there with meat and with fish, respectively.

There are those wine-lovers, however, with palates more delicate than mine, who would not approve of lemon-juice in any form, not even blended into a salad-dressing with the noblest of first-pressing olive oils.

For such dainty drinkers, let me commend the salad dressing compounded by that great wine-and-food man, Robin McDouall, sometime secretary of the Travellers' Club.

He mixes one part of a dry white wine with three of olive oil, and then with salt, pepper, and chopped herbs – garlic, parsley, tarragon and chives. (I should go easy with the garlic – up to the point at which it enhances the flavour of everything else, whilst yet self-effacing.)

Some there are, lucky enough to have little more important to occupy their minds, who concern themselves with the problem of what wine to drink with melon served as a first course.

My own views about melon (of which I am very fond) are

mixed: the sweet and truly flavoury melons, such as Ogen, Charentais and Israeli, I would as soon have at the end of the meal as at the beginning, with a sweet wine or with none.

The boring, tasteless honeydew is certainly not interesting enough for the end of a meal – if it should chance to be ripe enough to secrete a drop or two of juice, it is all right as an hors d'oeuvre with a good Parma ham or, better still, a San Daniele, but how often does one come across that delicacy outside northern Italy?

It was my idea, though Carlo of the Café Royal Grill Room now claims it as his own, that if a sweet, full-flavoured melon will go well as a first course with raw ham why not with smoked salmon* or with *bressaola*, which is dried salt beef, and a Valtelline speciality?

My own view is that a melon ready to eat is juicy enough not to need the accompaniment of a glass of wine and, if it did, sweet enough to demand a wine itself too sweet to be followed by the dry wines that have been ordered to go with the main course.

Honesty obliges me, though, to record that I have been taken out by a friend in the wine trade to a summertime luncheon that began with an ice-cold Charentais melon, full of juice, and with the most imperious scent and delicious flavour, partnered by a Quarts de Chaume, one of the light wines of the Loire, that was sweet enough and scented enough not to be overwhelmed by the sweet and scented melon, and yet not itself so overwhelming as to diminish the authority of the dry white burgundy that followed with the main dish, which was a lobster mayonnaise.

All the same, I still feel that although my wine-trade friend had demonstrated that the trick could be done – a double trick, indeed: a wine that would go with melon, and a sweet wine that could precede a dry – I was intellectually, but not emotionally, convinced: I enjoyed the combination, but I do not think that I would have repeated it myself when next I was a host.

---

* Parma and San Daniele hams are not smoked as salmon is, though in English menus they are usually referred to as 'smoked' ham: they are salted and fresh-air cured.

Many people pour port into melon, and I would as soon pour port into Stilton: I have read of an American doctor who uses a fine hypodermic to inject brandy or a sweet liqueur into melons, and the author who recorded this interesting surgical practice observed that he would like to try the operation with kummel.

I should not.

*   *   *

Oh, I almost forgot . . .
Never drink port with pickled onions – not even Liz's.

Liz

Poor Ray is always torn, as he admits, between claret and horseradish, and they are, indeed, incompatible.

Some combinations that are generally held to be so, though, can accompany each other quite happily.

For instance, all the good books say that it is impossible to drink wine with curry – only beer will do.

But we have dined in Bordeaux, Ray and I, with a most distinguished claret family – discriminating diners, too – and been served a fine first-growth Graves with curried prawns, which went very well together.

For there is as long a Franco-Indian as an Anglo-Indian tradition – Pondicherry was French until our own time, but the French, characteristically, use curry delicately, as a subtle spice, not as a fierce condiment, and dishes *à l'Indienne* are usually very mild, but quite delicious. Here is one of chicken:

CHICKEN IN CURRY CREAM SAUCE

Joint a young chicken and roll the joints in well-seasoned flour. Heat a mixture of oil and butter in a frying pan, add the chicken pieces, a finely chopped onion and a dessert-spoon of curry powder. Cook for about fifteen minutes until the chicken gets golden brown. Remove the pieces from the pan and keep warm. To the fat in the pan add a tablespoon of flour, stir well and cook for a few minutes before adding half a pint of warm milk. Cook this sauce until it thickens, season with salt and pepper, return the chicken to the pan and continue cooking until the chicken is quite tender. Just before serving, add two tablespoons of cream.

If you want to use cooked chicken, make the sauce with the onion and curry powder in the same way then add the chicken pieces and heat them thoroughly in it.

Chicken, 1; flour, salt; pepper; oil; butter; onion, 1; curry powder, 1 dessertspoon; milk, ½ pint; cream, 2 tablespoons

Let me put in a plea for vinegar, too. Not the harsh malt vinegar – which used to be called alegar in the old days – but the vinegar which is really *vin-aigre* or soured wine, for this can be used in many different ways and dishes. It is easy to make yourself, too, by adding to a bottle of wine vinegar all left-over wine, topping up the bottle as you get more left-overs of wine. The vinegar will keep on going, but in much milder form than the usual shop-bought brands.

One unusual way of using it, which I didn't really believe would work when I first heard about it (from Hedges and Butler, the Regent Street wine merchants, who ought to know about such things, and who use their own old sherry vinegar) is to marinade strawberries in it.

MARINADED STRAWBERRIES

The way to do this is to hull the strawberries, put them in a bowl with one or two tablespoons of sugar, and to every pound of strawberries pour over a tablespoon of wine vinegar, stir them in this then leave for several hours. If the strawberries are wanted for lunch, do them early in the morning, or if for dinner, do them at lunch time. This brings out the flavour of the strawberries in a remarkable way, and is particularly good for the first imported ones, or for slightly under-ripe fruit that hasn't got a great deal of flavour.

Strawberries, 1lb; sugar, 2 tablespoons; wine vinegar, 1 tablespoon

The only time I like to use malt vinegar is in making chutney or in vinegar-cake. This is a fruit-cake similar to the kind still served in many London clubs as Lunch cake, an after-luncheon pudding. It is not so rich as the usual fruit cake and contains no eggs; my father was allergic to eggs in any form, and our old cook, Grannie Goward, used to make it for him.

VINEGAR CAKE
Mix 1lb of flour, $\frac{1}{2}$lb of brown sugar; $\frac{1}{2}$lb of butter and 1lb of dried fruit – sultanas, currants, raisins, and a little candied peel if liked. Put a teaspoon of bicarbonate of soda into $\frac{1}{2}$ pint of milk and add three tablespoons of vinegar. This will froth up at once, and while still foamy add to the dry ingredients and mix well. Bake at once in a fairly hot oven (400° gas 6) for half an hour, then reduce oven heat to 325° gas 3 for a further hour and a half. Half quantities can be used as successfully.

Flour, 1lb; brown sugar, $\frac{1}{2}$lb; butter, $\frac{1}{2}$lb; mixed fruit, 1lb; peel, $\frac{1}{4}$lb; milk, $\frac{1}{2}$ pint; bicarbonate of soda, 1 teaspoon; vinegar, 3 tablespoons

Even though I use malt vinegar in chutney, I use wine vinegar for pickling onions: the result, although more expensive, is vastly worth while. The onions remain crisp and keep their oniony flavour, rather than just becoming a strong, sharp pickle. Like so many good recipes, this comes from Eliza Acton's *Modern Cookery*, first published in 1845. She obviously knew her onions!

PICKLED ONIONS

Take about half a pint of vinegar for every pound of onions.
Bring the vinegar to the boil with spices of your own choice,
such as peppercorns, allspice, coriander or a mixture of all,
and a good teaspoon of salt. Skin the onions – if you plunge
them into boiling water for a minute or so the skins come
off more easily – and put them into the boiling vinegar.
Boil them for two or three minutes, until they begin to look
clear, then put them into jars, pour the vinegar over them,
and when they are cold screw on the lids of the jars.

Mint sauce, as usually served, is a strong vinegary mixture
which quarrels, as Ray says, with fine wine. For those who
like the flavour of mint, but also like their wine, there are two
solutions. One is to chop mint and mix it with sugar and lemon
juice and leave for several hours to blend the flavours, and the
other is to put the mint into the gravy:

MINT GRAVY SAUCE

Pour off the excess fat from a roast lamb joint and scrape the
juices into a saucepan with a little water. Pour in a glass of
red wine, bring to the boil for a few minutes, then add at
least two tablespoons of chopped fresh mint. Thicken with a
teaspoon of arrowroot previously mixed with a little water.
    The same method can be used with different herbs for
different meats. Lamb goes well with rosemary, too, but the
spikes of rosemary are unpleasant to the mouth, so if doing
a rosemary gravy in this way strain the sauce before serving:
the flavour will remain.

Salad dressings vary with the salad and the taste of the salad
maker. The basic French dressing consists of salt, pepper,
garlic or mustard, and sugar if liked, one part of vinegar to
three parts of oil. Olive oil makes the best dressing, though it
is often too heavy (and expensive) to cook in, when the lighter
tasteless vegetable oils are better. Some people prefer more
vinegar to oil, but I find this makes the dressing too sharp for
my taste.

Tarragon vinegar makes a magic dressing for salad, and is easy to do if you have fresh tarragon. Simply put sprigs of fresh tarragon in a bottle, fill up with wine vinegar and leave. This can be used straight away, or will keep for a year until the next tarragon comes along, and for many dishes needing the flavour of tarragon a dash of this vinegar will be all that is needed. Other herbs can be used in the same way, but this is the most subtle in flavour.

One way of dressing a green salad that prevents its getting soggy, or swimming in unnecessary dressing, is to put the salad into a bowl, sprinkle it well with salt, then pour over two or three tablespoons of oil. Toss well so that each bit of the salad is coated, and only then add a drop or so, no more, of vinegar or wine to sharpen the oil. This way the oil protects the leaves so that the vinegar doesn't penetrate, causing limpness in the leaves. If you have been too lavish with the oil, remove the salad to another bowl before serving.

CHAPTER SEVEN

Befores and Afters and In-betweeners

IN ONE and the same chapter of Trollope's novel, *The Warden*, the Reverend Mr Septimus Harding, warden of Hiram's Hospital in Barchester, dines once in a London eating-house on a mutton chop and a pint of port, next day on a mutton chop and a pint of sherry.

How times have changed in the hundred and twenty years or so since *The Warden* was written! And not only because the chop house in the Strand charged Mr Harding only half-a-crown for his pint of sherry. (A pint is two-thirds of a full-sized bottle – between a bottle, that is, and a half-bottle.)

For the one thing, nowadays, that we do not ask either of these versatile wines to do is to accompany the main course of a meal.

Sherry we drink dry, as an aperitif; we drink it sweet as a dessert wine; we drink it with soup and even *in* soup; we drink it alone, with a biscuit, at mid-morning; and we drink it in company, with all sorts of titbits, at sherry parties – but we do not wash down mutton chops with it.

It is as well. For today's palates, sherry is both too concentrated in flavour and too strong (about half the strength of

neat whisky and about twice the strength of claret) to be drunk
as a table wine in the way that we drink claret or hock. It is a
wine to sip rather than to drink deep.

For sipping before a meal, the austere palate chooses a light,
dry Manzanilla, or a Fino, but the same drinker on a colder
evening, or after a tiring day, when the system needs sugar as a
pick-me-up, might well find the softer, nuttier, rather less dry
Amontillado more comforting.

This, I think, is also the sherry for sherry parties, where not
every guest would enjoy the driest wines.

Similarly, if the old-fashioned English custom – unnecessary,
but hospitable – is to be followed, of a glass of sherry with the
soup, I would suggest a Fino with a clear consommé, an
Amontillado with thick or strongly-flavoured soups.

It has been alleged against the British wine-drinker that
what he likes is 'dry on the label; sweet in the bottle', and it is
true that many of the most widely advertised sherries with
'dry' in their brand names – Dry Fly, Dry Sack and Bristol
Dry, for example – are not so dry as all that: they are *medium*
or even sweetish sherries, not dry enough for some as pre-
dinner drinks, but well-suited for a mid-morning break with a
biscuit.

The really sweet 'cream' or 'old brown' sherries are dessert
wines and, unlike port, will stand up pretty well to tobacco
smoke after dinner, though I think it a damned impertinence
to ask them to.

*   *   *

Twenty years or so ago, when I was merely middle-aged, Mr
Michael Flanders, white-tied and opera-hatted, used to get a
world of Edwardian wickedness into,

> *Have some madeira, m'dear,*
> *You really have nothing to fear,*
> *I'm not trying to tempt you, that wouldn't be right:*
> *You shouldn't drink spirits at this time of night . . .*

– not that there is anything particularly Edwardian or particularly wicked about madeira, save that it was said to be 'the

best wine in the world' by George IV who was, I suppose, wicked, and that an 1846 Bual was a favourite tipple of the last Tsar of All the Russias who was, in a manner of speaking, an Edwardian.

Throughout the long Victorian Sunday morning, it was the wine to go with a hospitable slice of madeira cake – so-called not for what it was made of but for what it went with.

It has more, though, to offer those who like it – which I do not – than the capacity to wash down a mouthful of cake-crumbs.

Like port and sherry, madeira is a fortified wine: spirit is added to check fermentation, preserve natural sweetness, and add strength. But it is matured in a way peculiar to itself – baked in hot ovens – and it may be this, or the volcanic soil of the island of Madeira, where its grapes are grown, or other undefined factors that give madeira its rich, almost caramelly, taste (not incompatible, in some madeiras, with an austerely dry undertaste) and its amazing longevity.

Nowadays, madeira is made like sherry, on the *solera* system, one year's wine being added in cask to previous years', but there are single-vintage, unblended madeiras still vigorously drinkable after a century and a half, and more.

I have myself drunk unblended madeiras of the years of Waterloo and of Trafalgar. That was on the island they come from, where they tell how Winston Churchill, visiting them after the war, to paint, was given an especially ancient wine over which he nodded his head, lost in thought, before booming over the table to his hosts, 'Do you realize, gentlemen, that when this wine was made' – an impressive pause – '*Marie Antoinette was still alive?*'

There are four main types – Sercial is the palest, nutty in flavour, with a mellow dryness and an almost bitter after-taste. It is the best for drinking before meals.

Verdelho is still dry enough for an aperitif, or with soup, but softer and richer enough to be drunk as a dessert wine. Bual and Malmsey are both luscious dessert wines.

There are madeiras styled 'Old Rainwater', which does not signify adulteration, but an old-fashioned way of fining and maturing the wine: it has always been a favourite of old Southern families in the United States.

But the heaviest drinkers of madeira are in Scandinavia, which takes more than half the island's output; the island itself is Portuguese; the growing and shipping of the wine is largely in British hands; and the most ecstatic paean in its praise was sung by a former London editor of the *Yorkshire Post*, the learned wine-lover Warner Allen, who wrote:

> Greatest of all Madeiras, Malmsey, in which great bottle-age transforms a quintessence of sweetness into a profound magnificence of ambrosial immortality such as the gods in the Golden Age drank in Olympus after they had quenched their thirst with nectar, is perhaps the finest wine in the world . . .

I cherish the sudden access of Yorkshire caution in the word 'perhaps' – and still, myself, consider madeira a cooking wine.

So, too, Marsala, from Sicily, which is the best of all wines to make one of the best of all puddings, zabaglione, which Italian brides (I am told) give to Italian bridegrooms on their honeymoons for who knows what reason. And Edward Lear – no honeymooner, he – wrote of himself that –

> *He sits in a beautiful parlour,*
> *With hundreds of books on the wall;*
> *He drinks a great deal of Marsala,*
> *But never gets tipsy at all.*

*   *   *

I am not much keener on port than I am on madeira, which is disloyal of me, for it has been the traditional wine for loyal toasts since the Hanoverian Georges decided to continue Queen Anne's patronage of Portuguese wines, and the Jacobites took to drinking the health of their Stuart 'King over the Water' in the wine of the country to which he had fled – claret. We drink our present monarch's health in port because she is a Hanoverian.

A series of Anglo-Portuguese commercial treaties ensures that the name, 'port', may be applied to wine from nowhere else but the mountainous upper reaches of the Douro, a stern country scorched by a cruel summer sun, foggy and frosty in winter, and blasted by quick local thunderstorms.

Normally, this is a country that would produce a full-bodied, coarse red table wine for its peasants, and it was such a wine, no doubt, that the Portuguese cod-fishers of the Middle Ages brought to English shores.

But when, because of the war of Marlborough's time with France, Portuguese wines were given a prohibitive preference over French, it became important to make the harsh, dry Douro wines palatable: brandy was added to arrest fermentation, and thus preserve the natural, fruity sweetness of the wine. Thus port was born – the strong, sweet, luscious, fortified wine that still brings the sunshine of the south in concentrated form to the chilly northerners for whom it was first confected.

To the minds and palates of most connoisseurs the greatest of all ports is vintage port: it is certainly the wine to which legend attaches itself – the wine of a particularly great year aged for two years in cask and anything from twelve to twenty in bottle, and a homogeneous miracle of strength and delicacy, sweetness and flavour.

Vintage port throws a heavy crust or sediment as it ages in bottle, so that it needs to be rested and needs, also, to be decanted. The cork is sealed with wax, which has to be chipped away beforehand, but without disturbing the contents. So there are those who fight shy of vintage port as being 'too much trouble', though any good wine-merchant, given a day's notice, will decant a bottle for you and send it round, bright and clear, with the old cork tied to the neck of the new bottle. Why keep a butler?

But there are distinguished alternatives to vintage port. The wine matures more quickly in wood than in bottle, and if port is kept for five or six years or so in cask, instead of for two, it will 'come on' more quickly, and also – most important of all – leave its sediment behind. This so-called 'late' bottled vintage port can be bottled 'bright' and handled easily and, not quite so noble a wine as the greatest vintage (always perhaps a little lighter, a little lacking in 'depth'), nevertheless it is the wine of a single year, from a great shipper, and one that any connoisseur may be offered, and with pride. So, too, with crusted port, which is good wine not of a vintage year, or perhaps a blend of more than one year, but treated in the same way as a vintage wine, matured in bottle, and needing to be decanted. Matured in cask, like a late-bottled vintage, a fine quality blended wine of this type would be called a vintage reserve.

Nobody, though, drinks ports such as these every day of his life, and they account for only a small proportion of the total volume of port that reaches these shores.

It would be a pity if the towering prestige of vintage port, whether bottled early or late, and that of old crusted port, should obscure the day-to-day virtues of this robust and versatile wine.

Ruby, for instance, a wine old enough in wood to have lost its youthful purple, but young enough to be rich and full – and the cheapest, for capital has been tied up in it for a shorter time – is the wine for everyday after-dinner drinking, to go with a biscuit on a winter's morning, or for mixed drinks and mulls, of which more later. As it is a blended wine – from different years and from various vineyards – shippers can maintain continuity of style in a ruby port, and those sold under famous brand-names will taste the same this year and next; at home, in a restaurant, or at the bar.

The same can be said of tawny, which has aged to a lighter colour than ruby, and is slightly drier, smoother, more elegant. There are notable wine-lovers who prize an old tawny higher even than a great vintage port for after-dinner drinking, and others who find that its nuttiness both of flavour and of fragrance make it an appetizing aperitif.

It may be that we take port too seriously in this country. In recent years, France has outstripped Britain as the Douro's biggest export market (not, though, for vintage port, virtually all of which comes to this country) because the French, having discovered Portugal as a cheap place for holidays, have discovered, too, the virtues of 'porto' as a between-meals drink, and are not overawed, as we are, by the age-old traditions and conventions that cling to the consumption of vintage.

Those cloth-capped old biddies were wise in their generation who used to call in working-class pubs for 'a port and lemon, dearie', for they were acknowledging, however unconsciously, that port generally (and ruby port in particular) has the colour, strength, and fullness of character and flavour to stand up to being diluted – or, indeed, iced or spiced or otherwise used as a base for long drinks, hot or cold, or for short, mixed, appetite-whetters.

The cloth-capped old biddies have gone, and so have many of their pubs, but rich, robust, ruby port remains, and responds handsomely to being taken as a long drink with tonic-water and ice, just as a tawny (though I should not choose the oldest and finest tawny) mixes with gin or with vodka, well-chilled, as a short.

Ruby in a long glass with ice, soda, and a slice of orange is a deliciously fruity cooler on a summer's day, and I have it from a member of one of the most famous of port-shipping families that when he was a young masher in Oporto in the 1920s, a mixture of port and fizzy lemonade, well-iced, was the sophisticated thing to serve at swagger lawn-tennis parties given by the British colony of those days. The same drink, in fact, that was regarded as a charwoman's tipple over here. I have had many a worse summer wine cup than this, served under fancier names.

Liz

Sherry, although more popular than either madeira or port as a drink, is not so much used in the kitchen, unless it is to fortify the cook herself. However, here are one or two recipes in which it is used, or for dishes to be eaten as a first course

with sherry as an accompaniment. The first one is from Elizabeth Raffald's eighteenth-century *Experienced English Housekeeper*, and bears the charming name of

A NICE WHET BEFORE DINNER

Cut some slices of bread about half an inch thick and fry them lightly in butter. Put them into the dish in which they are to be served and place an anchovy fillet on each slice. Mix together some grated Cheshire cheese and parsley then cover the bread thickly with this mixture. Dot with butter and brown under a hot grill so that the cheese melts. Serve as a first course. (If you think the anchovies may be too salty, marinade them for half an hour in milk.)

Bread, 4 slices; anchovy fillets, 4; cheese, 2–3oz; parsley; butter

A sherry sauce can serve to brighten up rather ordinary fish, such as cod or whiting fillets. A dry rather than a full sherry is best for cooking, unless for a particular dish that calls especially for a rich one.

FISH IN SHERRY SAUCE

Skin and cut into pieces one and a half pounds of white fish. Melt two ounces of butter with two tablespoons of milk and cook the fish gently in this until they are almost done. Add a teaspoon of lemon juice and finish the cooking. Remove the pieces of fish to a serving dish and keep warm. To make the sauce add another ounce of butter to what remains in the pan, mix in two or three tablespoons of cream, bring to simmering point and add a small glass of sherry. Finally thicken the sauce by adding a beaten egg yolk, but take care not to let it boil again. Pour the sauce over the fish, sprinkle with chopped parsley before serving.

Fish fillet, 1½lb; butter, 3oz; milk, 2 tablespoons; lemon juice, 1 teaspoon; cream, 2–3 tablespoons; sherry, 1 glass; egg yolk, 1; parsley

One of the all too many English dishes that can be rich and delicious or quite revolting is trifle. Too often, it is dry cake moistened with packet custard and oversweet jam. Properly made, though, it can be a party treat.

SHERRY TRIFLE (OR TIPSY CAKE)

First make a thick custard with two eggs, an ounce of sugar and half a pint of milk (see below). Cook until it thickens then let it cool. Cover the base of a deep bowl with a layer of sponge cake, and sprinkle this liberally with sherry. This is one case when a full bodied sherry can be used (or Madeira or Marsala) as you should be able to taste it. Cover the cake with a layer of jam. I prefer apricot as it is less sweet than some, and goes particularly well with the almond ratafia biscuits which should be put on top of the jam. Sprinkle this layer with more sherry, pour the thick custard over, then top with a layer of whipped cream and decorate with toasted almond flakes.

Sponge cake; sherry; apricot (or other) jam; ratafia biscuits; custard made with two eggs, 1 ounce of sugar and $\frac{1}{2}$ pint milk; whipped cream; toasted almond flakes

CUSTARD

Mix three ounces of sugar, preferably vanilla flavoured, with three egg yolks, or two whole eggs, and beat until they are thick and creamy. Bring a pint of milk to boiling point, pour a little onto the eggs and sugar to mix, then return the whole to the saucepan. Cook slowly, stirring all the time, until the mixture thickens enough to coat the back of the spoon, but do not let it boil. When it is thick, pour it into a shallow dish to cool. Cook the custard in the top of a double boiler, or in a bowl over boiling water if you fear that it will boil and curdle. It takes longer that way but is safer. If you want the custard thicker use less milk – or more eggs.

If you keep a vanilla pod in a jar of sugar it will flavour the sugar well and is much cheaper than buying ready prepared vanilla sugar, as the pod lasts for a long time. Another way

to flavour the custard is to infuse a vanilla pod in the milk as
it comes to the boil. Either of these ways gives a good but
subtle taste of vanilla, and both are preferable to using
vanilla essence.

Egg yolks, 3 (or whole eggs, 2); sugar, 3oz; milk, 1 pint

Another eighteenth-century recipe is for syllabub. Once
upon a time this would be made with sweet white wine, very
fresh milk (one recipe calls for the cow to be milked straight
into the wine and sugar) and would have been more of a
drink than a cream, but in this version the result is light and
fluffy and holds its shape in the glass, particularly if made the
day before it is needed, which also gives time for the flavours
to blend together well.

SHERRY SYLLABUB

Mix together the grated rind and the juice of a lemon with
two or three tablespoons of sugar, two glasses of sherry and
a little brandy. Stir until the sugar is dissolved. In a large
bowl put half a pint of thick cream and beat this until it
starts to thicken. Gradually add the sherry mixture, beating
the cream all the time until it is all incorporated and the
cream thick. Put into glasses and serve very cold.

Eliza Acton insists that no syllabub is good or wholesome
without brandy added, but if you haven't got any I doubt if
it would really matter, the sherry is what gives the flavour.

*Sherry, 2 glasses; lemon, 1; sugar, 2–3 tablespoons; cream
½ pint; brandy*

It is not always easy to give exact proportions for this kind
of dish as so much depends on the sweetness required, or the
sherry being used. One good thing about that, though, is that
the cook can keep trying it until the right blend is reached – if
by then there is any left.

Sherry is useful not only in giving flavour to dishes, but can
also act as a preservative. This recipe – again a traditional one –

is a good way of using up odd bits of cheese that are too dry or too small to serve in any other way. Made this way, cheese will keep for several weeks if sealed with clarified butter.

POTTED CHEESE

Mix three ounces of butter – unsalted if possible – with a pound of plain hard grated cheese. Add a small glass of sherry and half a teaspoon of spice, such as paprika and mace, or allspice and coriander, or what you like. Mix all this well together, in a mixer for ease and speed, until it becomes a soft mass. Put into small pots, press well down and seal with butter.

Cheese, 1lb; butter, 3oz; sherry, 1 glass; spices, ½ teaspoon

Orange jelly is an old English dish, traditionally served at Christmas, often served in the emptied halves of the orange. This is an old way of making it, with sherry or Marsala.

ORANGE JELLY

Take the rind thinly off four oranges and steep the peel in two or three tablespoons of Marsala or sherry. Dissolve half an ounce of gelatine in a little water, and dissolve a quarter of a pound of sugar in a quarter of a pint of hot water, then add the gelatine to this, also the juice and pulp of the oranges, with the juice of a lemon. Add the Marsala (having first removed the peel), turn into a mould or the emptied halves of oranges and leave to set.

Oranges, 4; water, ¼ pint; Marsala or sherry, 2–3 tablespoons; sugar, 4oz; lemon, 1; gelatine, ½oz

You can 'drink a great deal of Marsala and never get tipsy at all', or so we are told by Edward Lear, but this wine with its very distinctive flavour is best known in that delicious Italian dish of zabaglione, though I have suggested that it could be used instead of sherry in a trifle. Zabaglione is quick to make, but tricky to get the consistency absolutely right so that it doesn't separate if kept waiting. At the Gritti Palace in Venice they use a little gelatine to hold it, which means that it can be eaten cold instead of the usual way of serving it warm. It seems less rich when cold, so this is their version.

ZABAGLIONE GRITTI

Put into a bowl or the top of a double boiler six egg yolks, two and a half ounces of sugar, two and a half fluid ounces of marsala (or if you have no marsala use a full-bodied sherry). Dissolve half a packet ($\frac{1}{4}$oz) of powdered gelatine in a little warm water and add to the egg mixture. Put the bowl over a pan of hot water and beat constantly until the mixture thickens and rises – remember to use a bowl big enough to allow this to happen for the mixture will be about treble in size.

When it is thick remove the bowl from the heat and continue to beat for a moment or two longer until it is nearly cool, then pour into glasses or small bowls and let it get quite cold.

At the Gritti this is garnished with a blob of whipped cream and a little grated chocolate, or you can serve it as it is, but cat's tongues or lady's fingers go well with it. This is a rich sweet so this amount should be sufficient for four people or even six.

Egg yolks, 6; sugar, 2$\frac{1}{2}$oz; marsala, 2$\frac{1}{2}$fl.oz; gelatine, $\frac{1}{2}$ a packet ($\frac{1}{4}$oz); cream and grated chocolate as optional garnish

Ray's mention of port reminds me that some years ago we visited Oporto for the tercentenary of the firm of Warre & Co, and during the celebrations we had many local and delicious dishes, prepared by a remarkable lady called Maria do Ceu – Maria of the Heavens – who came from Lisbon but catered for parties all over the country, travelling with a refrigerated van, two cooks, two waiters and two portable stoves, and who provided enormous quantities of good food apparently with the wave of a magic wand. This was one of the dried cod dishes we had.

DELICIA DE BACALHAU

Soak the dried cod (*Bacalhau*) in water for twenty-four hours, changing the water at least twice. After it has soaked for this time, remove the skin and dice the flesh. Dice four or five potatoes and fry them lightly in olive oil until pale brown. Remove them from the pan and in the same oil fry the diced *bacalhau*. Remove this, and again in the same oil fry a finely chopped onion until lightly browned. Beat four eggs then scramble them in the same oil, then mix all the ingredients together and arrange in an ovenproof dish.

Make a thin béchamel sauce, add a spoonful of made mustard and pour over the fish and vegetable mixture in the dish. Grate some cheese, preferably Gruyère, over the whole, put the dish in a slow oven and bake for an hour.

Bacalhau (dried cod), 1½lb; potatoes, 4–5; onion, 1; olive oil; eggs, 4; béchamel sauce; mustard; gruyère cheese

Another speciality from Oporto is Tripe a Moda do Porto, a very substantial dish indeed, with tripe, chicken, beans and rice. On the only occasion we had it, we were advised to have one portion between two, and it was still too much.

TRIPAS A MODA DO PORTO

Clean and wash the tripe and calf's foot, cut into squares and cook in salted water until tender, which may take two or three hours. In another pan cook a quarter pound of dried beans (butter or haricot) until tender, and when nearly cooked add half a pound of smoked sausage, two chicken joints and a little smoked bacon. Cook for half an hour, then add three sliced carrots. When all the meat is tender, cut into small pieces, drain and reserve the liquid. In a large pan fry two chopped onions, then add the meat, tripe, beans and some parsley, a bayleaf, cumin seed and pepper. Moisten with about a pint of the reserved stock. Cook until blended together and the consistency of a stew. Cook four ounces of rice and serve separately.

Tripe, 1½lb; calf's foot, 1; smoked sausage, ½lb; chicken joints, 2; smoked bacon, ¼lb; beans (butter or haricot), ¼lb; carrots, 3; onions, 2; parsley; cumin; bayleaf; pepper; rice, ¼lb

The Portuguese seem to love rich sweet puddings, often made with lots of eggs – there is one called *Toucinho de Ceu*, which literally translated means Heavenly Bacon, but which is in fact an almondy custard, or Pudim Flan, another rather solid eggy dish, very sweet.

Two rather charmingly named sweet dishes are *Papos de Anjo* – Angel's Breasts – and *Sonhos* – Dreams.

PAPOS DE ANJO

Beat the yolks of five eggs until thick, then add the beaten white of one egg. Pour this mixture into small well buttered cake moulds and cook in a moderate oven for about twelve minutes until the egg is set.

Make a syrup with half a pound of sugar to a pint of water, and a strip of lemon rind. When this is cooked, re-move the custards from the tins, dip them in the syrup then place on a serving dish with the remainder of the syrup poured over them.

Egg yolks, 5; egg white, 1; sugar, ½lb; water, 1 pint; lemon rind

SONHOS

Put four ounces of butter and two ounces of sugar into half a pint of water and bring to the boil. Add five ounces of flour, mix in well and remove from the heat, then add four eggs one at a time, beating until the mixture is smooth. Leave to rest for ten minutes. Heat some oil in a deep pan and drop in spoonfuls of the batter and fry slowly until they are puffy and pale brown. Drain well on kitchen paper. Make a syrup with half a pound of sugar, half a pint of water and cinnamon to flavour. Serve the 'dreams' with the syrup poured over them while still warm, though the dish can be eaten hot or cold.

Butter, 4oz; sugar, 2oz; water, ½ pint; flour, 5oz; eggs, 4; oil for frying
Syrup: *sugar, ½lb; water, ½ pint; cinnamon*

The Portuguese taste for richly sweet pudding extends to Madeira, too, as on the only visit I have made there I was given this rather elaborate version of a crème caramel.

LEMON CARAMEL

Boil together four ounces of sugar with four tablespoons of water until they are caramelized, then coat the bottom and sides of a soufflé dish or mould.

Cream eight ounces of sugar with three and a half ounces of butter, then add the beaten yolks of six eggs and the grated rind and the juice of a lemon. Fold in the stiffly beaten egg whites, pour this mixture into the mould and bake in a *bain-marie* in a moderate oven (350° gas 3) for about three-quarters of an hour, or until an inserted knife blade comes out clean. Unmould when cold.

Sugar, 4oz; water, 4 tablespoons
Custard: *sugar, 8oz; butter, 3½oz; eggs, 6; lemon, 1*

This is very rich and sweet and you may wish to cut down on the sugar. Half quantities can be used successfully.

Not all the food in Madeira is sweet, though, and some of it is very simple. One flavoursome way they have of cooking meat is to use a bay twig as a skewer and they grill small pieces of meat on this like a kebab. In this way, the flavour of the bay permeates the meat.

Polenta or corn meal is used quite often, and this is sometimes fried as chips.

POLENTA CHIPS

Cook half a pound of polenta in a pint of salted water to which a little oil or lard has been added. Stir well and cook until it forms a thick porridge, and let this simmer for about an hour. Turn out on to a flat dish and leave to get quite cold. Cut into strips like chips, fry in hot oil until golden. They should be crisp outside with the centre soft.

Polenta, ½lb; water, 1 pint; oil; salt

A good dish, light but filling, is a tomato soup with poached egg that I was given at Reid's Hotel. You can leave out the egg and have the soup plain, but the egg and croûtons added make it a substantial enough dish for supper or lunch.

MADEIRA TOMATO SOUP

Slice a pound of onions thinly and cook them gently in a quarter pint of olive oil until they are soft but not brown. Put a pound and a half of ripe tomatoes into boiling water, skin them, then chop them roughly; add to the onions with a bayleaf, garlic, basil or marjoram, salt, pepper and half a pint of water. Continue to simmer until the vegetables are thick then blend to a purée. Allow an egg and a slice of bread for each person, then cut the bread into dice and fry crisp in oil; poach the eggs. Put the fried croûtons into the bottom of the soup bowls, pour on the hot soup and top with a poached egg.

If you wish to have the soup without the egg, use a little more water as the soup is very thick.

Onions, 1lb; tomatoes, 1½lb; olive oil, ¼ pint; bayleaf; garlic; basil or marjoram; salt; pepper; water, ½ pint; eggs, 4; bread slices, 4; oil for frying

One well-known dish connected with madeira is, of course, the madeira cake, so called not because it is made of madeira, or even comes from the island, but because it was the habit in the last century to eat a slice with a mid-morning glass of madeira, which goes very well with this plain cake.

MADEIRA CAKE

Cream half a pound of butter with half a pound of sugar, then beat in five eggs one at a time. Sift in half a pound of flour and beat until well mixed. Pour into a buttered and floured cake tin, sift caster sugar over the top and bake in a moderate oven for an hour. When the cake has just set, do not take it from the oven but put two or three thin slices of candied lemon peel on the top, then leave in the oven for the rest of the cooking time.

Butter, $\frac{1}{2}lb$; caster sugar; $\frac{1}{2}lb$; flour, $\frac{1}{2}lb$; eggs, 5; candied lemon peel

Madeira is a most useful wine to have in the kitchen. For one thing it gives flavour to a number of dishes, and even after the bottle has been opened its flavour doesn't alter, so although it

seems expensive initially it can last almost indefinitely. Use one of the drier ones such as Verdelho, not the rich heavy ones.

One way it is used is in this famous sauce.

MADEIRA SAUCE

Melt an ounce of butter and cook a finely chopped onion and carrot until golden. Season with a little salt and a pinch of sugar. Stir in a tablespoon of flour, cook for a few more minutes then add half a pint of stock, a tablespoon of tomato purée, parsley and a bayleaf and simmer until the sauce is reduced by about half. Strain the sauce, add a wine-glassful of madeira, simmer for five minutes and finish by adding half an ounce of butter.

Butter, 1½oz; onion, 1; carrot, 1; salt; sugar; flour, 1oz; stock, ½ pint; tomato purée, 1 tablespoon; Madeira, 1 wine-glass; bayleaf; parsley

Rather Harder Stuff

WHEN Dr Johnson said that 'he who aspires to be a hero must drink brandy,' it was tipsiness he was talking about not taste – he called claret the liquor for boys because, he said, 'a man would be drowned by it before it made him drunk,' and his tribute to brandy was that it 'will do soonest for man what drinking *can* do for him.'

No reader of mine, I am sure, turns to the brandy bottle to be done for in that sense, but many will echo the doctor's other good word for it, that 'the flavour of brandy is most grateful to the palate'. What that flavour is compounded of is essence of the grape – for brandy is the distillation of wine – and of years in oaken casks.

Any wine-growing country can make brandy, and most do: Italy, Germany and Spain all export sound brandies to this country. I have drunk some nice and some nasty brandies in Greece and a very good South African brandy in South Africa when I was permitted to visit that unhappy country – a visit I would not wish to repeat.

A really fine brandy from Soviet Georgia was served at our hotel in Kiev during Mr Macmillan's visit there in 1959. (It was the morning after a night out with my fellow-journalists on that Georgian brandy that I told my guide-interpreter – a nice but desperately earnest young woman – that no, I *didn't* want to be taken on a tour of a prize-winning collective farm with Mr Macmillan: what I wanted and what, indeed, I proposed to do, was to sit at a café table and watch the girls go by. My guide looked almost tragically reproachful: 'Mr Ray', she said, '*Oh*, Mr Ray! You are *very* light-minded'.)

Most people though who, with Dr Johnson, find the flavour of brandy grateful to the palate, think first of French brandy from Cognac and Armagnac, and of these two it is cognac that is by far the more commercially developed, and immensely the better known.

This is not the place to explain how brandy is made – many a text book will do that. (There is even rather a good one of my own, called, simply, *Cognac*.) Suffice it to say that brandy is distilled from a rather thin local wine and is, at first, crude and colourless. It takes on both colour and mellowness from the oaken casks in which it matures for at least five years, and the standard brands that are sold under such household names as Martell, Hennessy, Bisquit Dubouché, Rémy-Martin and Courvoisier are kept consistent as to their individual characters from year to year, and from bottle to bottle, by the judicious blending of the brandies of various vintages and the addition of a very little natural caramel made of burnt sugar.

Most of the great houses produce a 'three-star' brandy (Hennessy's is called Bras d'Or) suitable for long drinks such as brandy-and-soda. A drink I am fond of myself for occasional and in-between-whiles drinking – as a pick-me-up in the middle of a long morning, or at an interval in the theatre – is brandy-and-ginger-ale.

For drinking after dinner, as a liqueur, the older and softer VSOP (which stands for 'Very Special Old Pale') comes into its own. Rémy-Martin make nothing else; Martell's excellent VSOP is now called 'Medallion'; and some of the rather smaller firms make particularly fine VSOPs and even older liqueur brandies, notably Delamain – a great favourite of mine – Denis-Mounié, and Hine (which many an Englishman pronounces 'Eene', to show that he knows it to be a French firm, though the French pronounce it the English way, save for a little trouble with the aspirate).

Some respectable firms use 'Napoleon' as a trade-mark, or to denote age and quality, but there is no brandy on sale dating exclusively from the reign of either the first or the third Napoleon – if there were, it would be undrinkable. Famous houses that once labelled their brandies with the date of *the oldest element in a blend*, as it might be 1811 (mixed with much else), have discontinued this misleading practice.

The liqueur brandy you choose will be a matter of taste – armagnac tends to be fuller in flavour and darker than cognac and the cognacs vary according to whether they are three-star, VSOP or older, and as between the various firms.

At its best, brandy is superbly fragrant and, as the French well know, a notable digestive: no matter how noble a meal, brandy at the end of it makes it a better one, and better digested. And I have known it reconcile me and my stomach to many a culinary disaster.

Brandy, though, is not the only after-dinner digestive.

I do not know whether things are what they were, but the leaflet that used to accompany each bottle of Woodward's Celebrated Gripe Water, the Infant's Preservative, proudly quoted Nurse W. of Bristol: 'Was taken by Father for his abdominal pain with such relief that he now takes it for flatulence.'

Kümmel could have done as much for Father; for it, too, is compounded of caraway seeds and alcohol – rather more alcohol, I have no doubt, than in the Infant's Preservative, but then it costs three or four quid a bottle as against what we used to call shillings.

Nor is it the only liqueur to possess digestive properties: indeed, what we call liqueurs (and Her Majesty's Customs and Excise more prosaically describe as 'sweetened spirits') the French call digestives, suggesting smugly that they take for the good of their health what we paddle in from sheer self-indulgence, for the sake of their stained-glass colours, their taste or their smell.

Not, as a rule, that we give their delicious smell a fair chance. All too often they are served in glasses not much bigger than thimbles, filled to the brim. Try your Grand Marnier next time, or your Bénédictine, in amounts no greater, but served in a port or a sherry glass, only about a third or a half full, or in one of the very small brandy balloons, and dip your nose into the ethereal vapours in the top of the glass. Here is a great part of the pleasure to be derived from these pretty kickshaws.

I know there are those dedicated port-drinkers and brandy-fanciers who affect to despise all these liqueurs as mere liquid sweetmeats, but I must admit that now and again – perhaps when I have been too self-denying in the matter of sugar, sweets and puddings – that it is a sweeter liqueur that I fancy, and I have an especial affection, perhaps born of a nostalgia for Italy, for the strong, sweet, herby flavour of Strega, which comes from Benevento, in southern Italy (*strega* is Italian for 'witch' – Benevento is in mountainous witches', werewolves' and warlocks' country), and carries evocative overtones for all who have sipped it after dinner on warm, scented evenings under some Sorrentine arbour.

Strega is not unlike a cross between green and yellow Chartreuse (another favourite of mine).

Chartreuse is an aristocrat among liqueurs: the green is the stronger and the yellow the sweeter (and cheaper) – both are based on a vast assortment of fine herbs; and the really knowing thing is to mix the two. My old and late-lamented friend, Vyvyan Holland, who was Oscar Wilde's son, has told of how his father, visiting the monastery of Grande Chartreuse, asked the almoner the secret of the monks' serenity and happiness.

'One of green to two of yellow,' said the almoner.

Another mixture is 'B and B', now to be had in bottles, ready-blended and bottled by the Bénédictine people themselves, but nothing more complicated than half-and-half brandy and Bénédictine, for those who find Bénédictine by itself rather too sweet.

I can recommend the application of the same principle – of

cutting a herb or a fruit liqueur with an extra amount of its basic spirit to reduce the sweetness without impairing the flavour – to almost any liqueur. Thus, Drambuie with Scotch whisky and Irish Mist with Irish; brandy with cherry brandy or the delicious apricot brandies that come from the Netherlands.

Cherry brandy, though, and apricot brandy are not brandies in the truest sense. They are cordials, rather: sweetened and flavoured liqueurs.

True brandies – *eaux de vie* in the strictest sense – can also be made from fruit. The mash of the fruit is allowed to ferment, and alcohol is distilled from it: this spirit will be dry, because the sugar of the fruit has been fermented out, and unless it is then aged in casks, taking on colour from the wood, it is as colourless as water – as, indeed, whisky would be, were it not aged in cask.

An exception is calvados, the apple brandy of Normandy – the only one of France's fruit-brandies to be aged in wood, so that it takes on a honey-coloured or a tawny tint. This great drink comes from just beyond the northern most frontier of Europe's wine-growing region, and two other famous fruit-brandies come from outlying parts of it – slivovitz, the plum brandy of Yugoslavia and other Balkan countries, and barack palinka, Hungary's potent but highly palatable apricot brandy.

These apart, virtually all the great classic fruit-brandies come from one geographical region: the upper reaches of the Rhine and the high upland country on its either side – from the Swiss countryside between Basle and the river's source in Lake Constance; from the Alsatian plain and the deep valleys of the Vosges on the French side; and from the Black Forest on the German.

The best-known, I suppose, is the one made originally from the wild black cherry of the region, but increasingly from cultivated cherries of the same sort – the brandy that may be referred to in Germany as Schwarzwaldischer kirschwasser, as coming from the Black Forest, in Switzerland as Basler kirschwasser, for it comes from near Basle, but in Alsace and the world at large as kirsch, simply, a godsend to fruit salad, and a noble after-dinner drink in its own right.

All these great fruit-brandies (with the exception of calvados and, sometimes, slivovitz), are colourless because they are matured not in wood but in wax-lined casks, in earthenware, or in glass: the taste of wood would detract from the flavour of the fruit. And it is this flavour, combined with the clean, utterly uncloying lack of lusciousness, that makes them such superb drinks for after dinner, and especially after heavy dinners of rich food.

Not that all the people that make them drink them in that way. In Germany, especially, they are drunk as schnapps, before a meal – many a Black Forest dinner, for me, has begun with paper-thin slices of Schwarzwaldischer smoked ham and a glass or so of the kirschwasser of the region, and my hosts have been surprised that I chose to go back to the kirschwasser with the coffee afterwards, where they would have drunk cognac or a sweet liqueur.

And it is different again in Normandy, where the time-honoured way to drink calvados is not so much before or after a meal as in the middle, to make a *trou Normand* – a 'Norman hole' – in the course of a heavy meal, to 'cut' the richness and to give renewed appetite for what is still to come.

Indeed, it is perhaps significant that these clean, uncloying, appetising fruit-brandies are the products of regions notorious for their heavy meals – Normandy with its heavy cream sauces, and Alsace with its choucroute.

Outside the areas of production those most likely to be found, after kirsch and framboise, calvados, and slivovitz, are two plum brandies, both probably from Alsace – quetsch, distilled from the small, purple 'switzen' plum; and mirabelle, from a sweeter, golden plum. These have a more subtle, less emphatic flavour than either kirsch or framboise, and there are some connoisseurs who esteem them more highly for that very reason, with mirabelle perhaps slightly the more highly regarded of the two.

I must confess, myself, to a liking for the much more assertive flavour of the brandy made from William pears, of which the best examples, it is generally agreed, come from Switzerland, and are known as Poire Williams, or Williamine.

If I drank this pear brandy often, it may well be that I should tire of its emphatic quality – its fragrance can be quite overwhelming – and turn to the more reticent, more subtle, flavours and fragrances of quetsch and of mirabelle. But I do not drink it often enough: part of the charm of all these exquisite essences of fruit is their infrequency.

But only a part: the rest of it is their intensity.

I was quoted again in Pseuds' Corner for writing in a magazine article that

> ... drink kirsch or quetsch of Williamine after dinner, and you can smell – even before you taste – that you have an orchard, a Black Forest hill-side, or a valley of the Vosges encapsulated in the glass you are cupping in your hand. Few other drinks are so evocative.

But I was unrepentant, and wrote to *Private Eye* as follows:

> That's the second time, damn it, that you have dragged me into Pseuds Corner, along with a quotation from one of my *Observer* articles on wine. You have me unnerved. I begin to feel unable to dip my beak into a bumper of burgundy without glancing over my shoulder to see whether a *Private Eye* private eye waits to clobber me for any observation more high-flown than that the stuff is dry or wet, red or white.
>
> If you dedicated yourself, as I do, to getting stoned in the service of your paper, you too, sir, might feel as I do, after a kirsch, a quetsch and a Williamine, that you had an orchard encapsulated in the glass you are cupping in your hand instead of whatever it is (or they are) that you usually cup in your hand after dinner.
>
> Pray, sir, let me be to continue my mopping-up operations with rod, gun and corkscrew in darkest Dipsomania. It is an arduous task, made none the easier if my morale is undermined by ill-informed criticisms from stay-at-homes.

*   *   *

This country has never been especially enterprising in making dry fruit brandies, and I can't think why, for we have the apples for an English calvados, the plums for slivovitz, the raspberries for framboise, and so on. But we do make one or two sweet liqueurs – Grant's is a good English cherry brandy, and Hawker's sloe gin is delicious. The cherry and apricot brandies of such Dutch houses as Bols and De Kuyper are as famous as any French liqueurs – but I can also recommend the Yugoslav Maraska, named after the Dalmatian district where the bitter cherries come from that gave maraschino its name. It is not so easy to find as some liqueurs I have mentioned, but retailers can get it from those shippers that import Yugoslav rieslings.

As we have talked of English liqueurs, let me pass on my recipe for a delicious damson gin that can be made at home. Divide among enough Kilner jars to take it, a mixture of four pounds of ripe damsons, a pound of caster sugar and three bottles of gin. Wipe, but do not wash the damsons, and cut deeply round their middles. Screw the jars tightly and shake every day for at least three months, after which the liqueur should be drained off and bottled – it is fruity but dry, not at all sickly sweet, and has a lovely plum colour and flavour.

There are enough different liqueurs to keep us all tiddly for a lifetime, and I must not forget the delicious liqueurs that are based on orange, such as Grand Marnier and the Italian Aurum; the American Southern Comfort, which is made of bourbon whisky and peaches, is immensely strong, and now available in this country; and Forbidden Fruit, also American, is made of brandy and a special breed of grapefruit, and put in the fanciest of bottles, shaped and ornamented like a royal orb.

Liqueurs are expensive, I know, but they can be bought in half-bottles and even in miniatures, and they keep indefinitely after being opened, so that they can be used economically. Do not forget when you are coming back from a holiday abroad that the duty saved is enormously more than on a bottle of wine.

In the course of a year, if each member buys half-bottles of different liqueurs, a sizeable family can accumulate quite an assortment in this way, and I can think of few more satisfying souvenirs than a tray with an assortment of different and differently coloured liqueurs appearing with the coffee after dinner, gleaming like jewels.

Better than straw hats and models of the Leaning Tower of Pisa.

Liz

Brandy and liqueurs are far less used in the kitchen than either table or fortified wines, though brandy finds a good home in the Christmas pudding or in mincemeat, which it helps both to keep and to flavour. And of course Brandy Butter is perhaps the best thing about the Christmas pudding. This is similar to the American Hard Sauce, and can be made with rum instead.

BRANDY BUTTER
Cream half a pound of butter, then beat in the same amount of caster sugar, add a good glass of brandy, a squeeze of lemon juice, and flavour with nutmeg and cinnamon.

Brandy, 1 glass; caster sugar, 8oz; butter, 8oz; cinnamon and nutmeg. The amount of sugar can be adjusted to taste

RUM BUTTER

This is made in the same way as the butter above, but pale brown sugar is often used instead of the caster.

Although I have yet to discover why these are called Brandy Snaps as they seem to have no connection, the name anyway makes it appropriate to give a recipe here. In my childhood we called them Jumbles, though I believe this name is usually given to the same mixture baked flat and not curled into tubes.

BRANDY SNAPS

Put two ounces of butter, two ounces of Demerara sugar, and two ounces of syrup into a pan and bring to the boil for five minutes. Add half a teaspoon of lemon juice and a little vanilla, and two ounces of flour. Put strips of this mixture on a floured and greased baking tray, leaving room between them for the mixture to spread during cooking. Bake in a moderate oven until lacy and golden. Let them stand for a minute then curl them quickly round the handle of a wooden spoon. When they are cold fill them with whipped cream. Or take them from the oven as they are and leave them flat, in which case you eat them without cream.

Butter, 2oz; brown sugar, 2oz; flour, 2oz; syrup, 2oz; lemon juice; vanilla (If preferred, use vanilla sugar instead of brown)

Brandy is often used to flambé dishes; again, Christmas pudding is the obvious example. Other spirits can be used the same way. What one must remember, though, is that the spirit does not easily burn unless it is warm. So put it in a small saucepan to heat up first, or in a heated spoon, then set light to it when it will fire easily and can be poured over the dish it is to enrich.

Here is one dish in which it is used, but in this case, as the flavour is of juniper, gin can be used instead.

JUNIPER QUAIL

Allow two quail per person, brown the birds in butter, and sprinkle with salt. Cover and simmer on top of the stove or in a moderate oven (350; gas 4) for twenty minutes. Add half a cup of stock, four or five crushed juniper berries and a glass of brandy. Continue to cook for another ten minutes.

Quail, 8; butter, 2oz; salt; stock, ¼ pint; juniper berries; brandy

Liqueurs are immensely useful in the kitchen, and need not be expensive, for if you have no particular need for a large bottle a miniature or two are usually sufficient for most purposes. The orange-flavoured liqueurs such as Cointreau or Grand Marnier are probably the most useful, having a distinctive taste as well as being sweet, while cherry brandy is not only a warming drink, but makes the easiest sweet dish of all, with a good flavour and pretty colour.

CHERRY BRANDY SYLLABUB

Beat a quarter pint of cream until it thickens slightly then mix in one or two tablespoons of cherry brandy and beat again. Sweeten if necessary, but if the cherry brandy is one of the sweeter brands the mixture will probably be all right as it is. Anyway, this is one of the dishes that are strictly to taste, so the cook can please herself, and taste as she goes along.

Cream, ¼ pint; cherry brandy, 1 or 2 tablespoons; sugar to taste

LIQUEUR CUSTARD

This can be flavoured with whatever liqueur you have by, but the stronger the taste the better.

Mix together ½ pint hot milk, small pinch salt, 2 tablespoons sugar and 3 tablespoons of liqueur, such as yellow or green Chartreuse or Cointreau (you name the custard after the liqueur it is based on). Beat together 4 egg yolks with 2 tablespoons cream and pour on to this the milk mixture, stirring very well. Return to a thick saucepan and cook gently over a low heat until the custard thickens, but do not let it boil. Pour into custard cups and let it get quite cold before serving.

Milk, ½ pint; pinch salt; sugar, 2 tablespoons; liqueur, 3 tablespoons; egg yolks, 4; cream, 2 tablespoons

Brandy is a delicious preservative of fruits – if you wish to preserve plums, cherries, peaches or what you will, the method is the same.

FRUIT IN BRANDY
Arrange the sound fruit in layers with caster sugar in glass jars. Fill up with brandy, cork tightly, shake well and keep for a month before using.

Frankly, I consider *crêpes Suzettes* a crashing bore – perhaps Suzette was? – and so I give here a recipe for a liqueur-based pudding that is not only more impressive, but more scrummy.

SOUFFLÉ GRAND MARNIER
Separate the yolks and whites of five eggs, putting one yolk aside. Beat the other four yolks with two tablespoons of sugar until they are thick and light. Cook this mixture in the top of a double boiler until it is thickened, then remove from the heat and beat until cool. Stir in two or three tablespoons of Grand Marnier. Beat the egg whites until stiff, fold them into the yolks. Pour into a soufflé dish prepared with a collar of paper round it so that it holds the rising soufflé, bake in a preheated hot oven for fifteen minutes, sprinkle with sugar, remove the paper collar and serve at once.

Eggs, 5; sugar, 2 tablespoons; Grand Marnier, 2 or 3 tablespoons

Grand Marnier makes its appearance, too, in duck with orange sauce. In too many English restaurants the sauce is too sweet and sticky, quite destroying the flavour of the duck, but this recipe, from M. Coolen the *patron-chef* of the Hotel

Clement at Ardres, near Calais, is all that it should be – rich, savoury, but neither too sweet nor cloying.

ORANGE SAUCE FOR DUCK

Make a brown *roux* with an ounce of butter and an ounce of flour, cooked to a warm brown. Squeeze the juice from five or six oranges (so that you have half a pint of juice) and keep an extra orange in reserve. Add two tablespoons of Grand Marnier and a tablespoon of curaçao (Cointreau is the best known) to the juice together with a quarter pint of stock, and season well with salt and pepper. Mix with the roux and cook gently until the mixture thickens. Cut the peel from the extra orange into very thin strips, add it to the sauce together with a little caramel colouring. Carve the roast duck into neat pieces, cover with the sauce and garnish with the flesh of the extra orange cut into segments.

Flour, 1oz; butter, 1oz; orange juice, $\frac{1}{2}$ pint; orange, 1 whole; Grand Marnier, 2 tablespoons; Curaçao, 1 tablespoon; stock, $\frac{1}{4}$ pint; salt; pepper; caramel for colouring

I see that Ray makes no mention of rum in this chapter, though I fancy that he mixes some drinks with it in Chapter 9. This, however, seems the appropriate place for rum as an accompaniment to fruit – and to none better than its compatriot, the banana.

BANANAS WITH RUM

Peel the bananas, cut them in half longways and cook in a little butter and brown sugar in a shallow pan until the fruit is soft. Heat a tablespoon of rum, light it and pour it over the bananas, shaking the pan until the flame dies down. Alternatively, the bananas can be baked in the oven with the rum.

Bananas; brown sugar; butter; rum

And, finally, a word for a couple of the fruit eaux-de-vie, much neglected, to my mind, in English kitchens:

PINEAPPLE AND ORANGE

Maraschino or kirsch are often used with pineapple, and a good way to serve this is to cut a pineapple in half lengthways cutting through the leafy top as well. Scoop out the pulp from each half of the pineapple making two shells, each with a leafy end. Dice or mash the pulp, mix with segments of orange, return the fruit to the shells and sprinkle with sugar and kirsch or maraschino.

Pineapple; oranges; sugar; kirsch or maraschino

CHAPTER NINE

Coolers-down and Warmers-up

'S UMMER drinks should be like summer girls', a writer in a wine-trade magazine once observed: 'long, cool, and half-full of gin . . .'

I cannot agree.

Five foot three myself, I see no reason for summer girls (or spring, or autumn, or winter girls, come to that) to be particularly long; I am not so keen on cool girls as on girls positively incandescent; and I found, in my unregenerate undergraduate days, that they were less likely to reach that interesting condition on gin (which makes some damsels merely morose) than on fizz.

For me, though, fizz is a cooler – always ice-cold, whether by itself, or served with half as much fresh (*not* tinned or frozen or bottled) orange-juice, when it may be called 'Buck's Fizz', 'Champagne-Orange' or 'Mimosa', according to whether you want to suggest familiarity with a particular London club, the cafés of Paris, or Giuseppe Fontana's admirable bar at the Gritti Palace Hotel in Venice.

Nor must I forget that it was the shipper of a most distinguished *marque* who, pooh-poohing the notion that champagne was too dignified a wine for dilution, told me that there was nothing he found more refreshing during a real scorcher than a long glass of bubbly, as cold as can be, with a bruised sprig of mint in it. I have asked for this on hot days in more than one smart West-End restaurant, sometimes successfully, sometimes eliciting astonishment that a bar or a kitchen should be expected to lay hands on a sprig of fresh mint.

Whatever the poet may say, though, life is *not* mostly froth and bubble ...

A. P. Herbert's advice was,

> Start her on champagne, boy,
>   but break her into hock –
> That's the only rule of life
>   that's steady as a rock.

going on to recall that he'd

> ... seen so many promising entanglements decline
>   Cos the lady weren't contented
> with a nice still wine.

So, if price is a problem, almost any dry Loire wine served cold makes a pleasant mouthful on a hot day; more refreshing than most hocks, to my mind, because of the greater acidity. And if the lady is a teetotaller – there are such – one of the best of all warm-weather drinks is one of the unsweetened apple juices, such as Shloer or Bulmer's, with a lump of ice and a slice of lemon in it.

It may be noticed that I have not gone in for any very elaborate mixtures. I cannot be bothered with all those preliminaries of peeling and measuring, and in any case I am far from fond of those wine-cups that consist of disintegrating tinned fruits sinking sadly into wash-basins of watered-down wine.

Here, though, for those who favour the fancier concoctions, are some recipes for mixed summer drinks (wine-, spirit-, and otherwise-based) that can not only refresh but invigorate. The secret with all such is to put as little ice as possible *into* the mixture or, better still, to do without it altogether by using a refrigerator, an ice-bucket, or one of those jugs or carafes with a separate ice-container.

For Badminton Cup, for instance, which is more likely to have been named after the Duke of Beaufort's desirable messuage than after battledore-and-shuttlecock, you pour a bottle of lightish red wine (they used to say claret, but a Valpolicella or the like would do) over half a cucumber, peeled and sliced, adding the juice of a lemon, a pinch of nutmeg, half a glass of any orange liqueur, and sugar to taste. When the sugar is dissolved, add a bottle of soda water, and ice (if you cannot do without it in one of the ways suggested).

Then there is a recipe I gave many years ago in a book that nobody read, and fewer still bought. My comment was that it was expensive, reassuring and refreshing, and not for young things unless you had designs on them. And I should like it to be known as Cyril Ray's Swagger Sling.

No expert knowledge required – you simply take a bottle of claret in one hand and a bottle of champagne in the other (it doesn't matter which hand) and pour them simultaneously into a big bowl. Add one glass of brandy and one of an orange liqueur – doing the thing in the style it deserves calls for Grand Marnier – the zest of a lemon, soft sugar to taste and no water, no ice, but serve as cold as you can.

'One of sweet, two of sour, three of strong and four of weak', which is to say one part of an orange liqueur, two of lemon juice, three of whisky, and four of soda water, – is the mnemonic for whisky punch. Decorate with fruit if you must, or with mint if I am your guest, and let us drink it, ice-cold, through straws.

I have imbibed variations on this theme – stingers, juleps, and the like – in North and in South America, and in Cyprus the brandy sour is virtually the national drink, one version or another of which has kept me company in that lovely island's happy and in its troubled times.

I say 'one version or another', because where three or four Cypriots are gathered together there are four or five different recipes – it is only fairly generally agreed that there should be two parts of brandy to one of bottled lemon squash, a dash or so of bitters, ice, a slice of lemon, and the lot made into a longish drink with soda water.

Some add sugar, which I think unnecessary with bottled squash, and if the drink is to be truly sour and thus refreshing; some encrust the rim of the glass with sugar, which is at once pretentious and uncomfortable; some add a bright red 'cocktail' cherry from a bottle, and it shall not be forgiven them.

And for 'Bull's Eye', you mix a pint of cider, a pint of ginger ale and a small glass of brandy – what could be simpler?

Now that so noble a drink as shandygaff – which used to consist of draught beer and ginger-beer, half-and-half – has become a little beer to a lot of fizzy lemonade sold in tins and called shandy, I turn instead to a mixture of a quart of brown ale with a wine-glass apiece of sherry and brandy, the peel and the juice of one lemon, a tablespoon or so of sugar and a pinch of nutmeg. In this case, a very little ice doesn't hurt.

Finally, let no one, please, write to ask me how much sugar, how juicy a lemon, how big a wine-glass. No recipe for a mixed drink is sacred, but should be adjusted according to taste. The thing to do is to go on experimenting beforehand until it doesn't matter a damn whether the guests turn up or not.

*   *   *

We got ourselves into that state, I recall, one blissful weekend – my wife, my secretary, a delightful girl from Penguin Books, a couple of other guests and I – devising a mixed drink with which to launch Penguin's publication of Scott Fitzgerald's *The Great Gatsby*, to coincide with the release of the film, in 1974.

The girl from Penguin Books insisted that there should be champagne in it, for the book – and Gatsby, and Scott Fitzgerald in his time – was full of it; I felt that there must be a truly American ingredient, and proposed that deliciously potent liqueur, Southern Comfort; bitters were needed to cut the sweetness a little, and as Southern Comfort is based on

peaches as well as bourbon it seemed proper that they should
be peach bitters.

It was hitting upon the right proportions that kept us occu-
pied from before dinner on the Friday until bedtime on the
Sunday, by which time I was sufficiently sloshed to christen my
creation 'Fizz-Gerald'.

As printed in the invitation to the publication party, it read
as follows:

Into an eight-ounce wine-glass put one thick slice of orange
and drop on to it 6–8 drops of peach bitters.
Add one jigger, or the bottle-cap full (about half a fluid
ounce) of Southern Comfort, and fill the glass with champagne.

I left before the party was over, but was told later that at one
in the morning the prettiest guest was under a table – and not
without companionship.

The creation of Fizz-Gerald was not the first such service I
performed for Penguin Books. Ten years or so ago, for the
25th birthday of their Puffin publications for children, that
great and good woman, Kaye Webb, their editor, persuaded
me to devise a celebratory cup. It consisted, in the end, of
sauternes, champagne, brandy, rosé and the particular kind of
Chambéry vermouth that is flavoured with wild strawberries,
in what proportions I have long forgotten, but it seems that
Kaye Webb has not, for she has been serving it, I am told, every
year since at annual parties for Puffin authors.

It is called Puffin's Pleasure, and – weak as are all authors in
their dealings with publishers – I never thought of asking for
a royalty . . .

*   *   *

If cups can cool, mulled wine can do much to mitigate the
miseries of a winter's evening, and one does not need to throw
a party as an excuse for making it: it is all so easy.

The classic *vin chaud* served in most French cafés in the winter
consists of nothing more elaborate than a bottle of red wine
(the cheapest will do), warmed up gently, and not allowed to

boil, with about half as much water, a sherry glass of brandy, sugar to taste – probably a couple of lumps – a pinch or two of cinnamon or nutmeg, and a slice of lemon to float on each glass.

The only basic rule about mulls is that wine should be heated gently, never boiled, and the necessary equipment is equally simple – a saucepan; glass mugs with handles, for mulls should be too hot to hold in a thin wine-glass; a spoon in each glass to prevent its cracking; some sort of hotplate on which to stand the jug or bowl, and a ladle.

The Austrians make *gluehwein* in much the same way as the French make their *vin chaud*, but omit the water – perhaps because they use a rather lighter red wine, such as the Italian Valpolicella, which they import in great quantities. And they are more likely to spice the concoction with cloves than with cinnamon.

A lordlier Viennese hot drink is called *Lebensretter*, or life-saver, and I should think so, too: a bottle of port to half a bottle of brandy, no less, mixed, sugared to taste, and served very hot. I have often given this recipe, and have had no complaints: perhaps those who tried it are still speechless.

A much more modest brew is negus, named not after the Emperor of Abyssinia but after a Colonel Francis Negus of Queen Anne's time. He added boiling water to an equal quantity of port, with sugar, lemon juice and lemon peel to taste, and has no other claim to fame whatsoever. But there have been worse reasons for a name becoming immortal.

Of the other fortified wines, madeira makes a good strong mull if you add a small glass of brandy to each bottle, with sugar to taste and whatever spices you fancy – cinnamon and ginger go well – and serve very hot.

One never hears of mulled sherry, as such, but I have come across a modified English version of the Swedish glögg that mixes a bottle of medium sherry, as it might be an amontillado, with a bottle of red wine, half a bottle of brandy, with cloves and cinnamon or with a few dashes of Angostura, sweetened to taste and warmed. Traditionally, there should be a couple of raisins and an almond in each glass.

White wine can be mulled, too, though it seldom is: some

years ago, Harveys of Bristol gave the recipe in their wine-list for what they called Harvey's Specifick – a large glass of brandy to a bottle of dry white wine, the juice of a lemon and half-a-dozen dessertspoons of honey, heated. It was recommended as 'an efficacious remedy against rheums and the ague', which may or may not be the case, but I can imagine it as reconciling one to a creaking joint or so.

Many people think of, and use, 'mull' and 'punch' as more or less interchangeable terms. Even the late, great Raymond Postgate, who was seldom wrong about anything, from Greek texts to significant dates in the history of the trade-union movement, actually wrote that 'hot wine' is 'usually called punch'. It is not. Hot wine is a mull, and punches, strictly speaking, are spirit-based.

There are exceptions, though, to the general rule that they are served cold. I dislike almost everything I have ever heard of that bloody-minded, reactionary bully, George Saintsbury (he advocated the shooting of conscientious objectors and coal-miners on strike), but I have always relished his comment on a hot punch that consisted of three of rum, two of brandy, one of lemon juice, six of hot water, and sugar to taste. 'I never knew this mixture found fault with', he observed, 'by respect-able persons of any age, sex or condition, from undergraduates to old ladies, at any hour between sunset and sunrise.'

And of rum toddy – hot rum-and-water with sugar, simply – he wrote: 'You must take it in bed: premature consumption merely wastes the good creature. It should be made, in a large rummer-glass, as hot as you can drink it (hence the advice of the rummer – for a mere tumbler may burn your hands), not too sweet, but so strong that you sink back at once on the pillow, resigning the glass to the ready hands of a sympathizing bedside attendant, preferably female.'

(Which reminds one again of Raymond Postgate's 'plump, pretty and rather greedy young woman', with whom to drink sauternes. Dear me, these wine-writers!)

Another hot rum drink uses tea instead of water – it is usually made by the glass. Pour a tot of one of the dark, heavier rums, such as Jamaica, into a half-pint glass mug, adding a tablespoon of lemon juice, a teaspoon or so of sugar to taste, and fill up with hot, weakish, Indian tea.

Or, using hot water instead of tea, put in three or four cloves and float a piece of butter the size of a walnut on top, stirring it gently until it dissolves. You then have hot buttered rum, which many Americans enjoy greatly, and I do not.

There is a long history behind a hot mixture of butter and ardent spirits. An officer on General Wade's staff in the Highlands in the 1720s wrote to a friend in London (so Professor David Daiches records, in his classic book, *Scotch Whisky*) that the Highlanders sometimes mixed their 'usky', which they drank 'without moderation', with water and honey or with milk and honey, but sometimes with sugar and butter: 'This they burn till the Butter and Sugar are dissolved.'

These, though, are grogs, and it is well to return to punches

proper which, as I have observed, are usually served cold.

One of the most famous of all cold punches is Philadelphia Fish-House Punch, said to have originated in 1732 in a Philadelphia club of that name. There are many versions, but the classic is to be found in 'Professor' Jerry Thomas's famous *How to Mix Drinks, or the Bon Vivant's Companion*, published in New York in 1862.

Having called for a quarter of a pint of peach brandy, half a pint of cognac, a quarter of a pint of Jamaica rum, a third of a pint of lemon juice, three-quarters of a pound of sugar and two-and-a-half pints of cold water, the 'Professor' observes, simply, that this 'is generally sufficient for one person'. So I should suppose.

And one of these days I shall get around to making the Punch Jelly, based partly, at any rate, on cognac and old Jamaica rum, which Jerry Thomas strongly recommends, with only this proviso, 'that many persons, particularly of the softer sex, have been tempted to partake so plentifully of it as to render them somewhat unfit for waltzing or quadrilling after supper'.

But when the day comes that I do make it, I shall ensure that it is served in plentiful supply. Anything to stop all that damned quadrilling by the softer sex after supper.

CHAPTER TEN

Glasses and Decanters

WHEN Bertrand Russell was seventeen, in 1889, he found himself by chance the only male in the Russell house hold at Pembroke Lodge when Mr Gladstone came to dine and stay the night.

Mr Gladstone was eighty years old, had been prime minister three times and was to be prime minister yet again. After dinner, the ladies retired and young Russell, himself the grandson of a prime minister, was left alone with the Grand Old Man. He waited for the pearls of political wisdom that would fall from those awesome lips.

There was a silence that the boy feared to break, and then, 'This is a very good port they have given me, but why have they given it me in a claret glass?'

Nearly eighty years later, when he was ninety-five years old, Russell wrote that, 'I did not know the answer, and wished the earth would swallow me up. Since then I have never again felt the full agony of terror.'

It was wrong of the old gentleman so to terrify his young host: a claret glass for port will do very well, for it need not be more than half-filled and that leaves room to dip one's nose into the smell of the wine, held in the top half of the glass. What would have been wrong would have been claret in a port glass – No room! No room! as they cried out at the Mad Hatter's tea-party (where there was no wine either, come to that . . .).

Some things matter about what you drink your wine from, some do not.

Try the wine you like best out of a glass and then out of a chipped enamel mug. For that matter, champagne tastes very different in a glass from the way it tastes in the silver mugs they use for it in some old-fashioned London clubs.

This does not mean that wine glasses need be very fine and very expensive (though very fine glass is nice to have).

What is important is that the glass should be reasonably thin and colourless. There should be a stem so that, when it holds cool white wine, the wine is not warmed by being cradled in your hand.

It should narrow towards the brim, becoming tulip-shaped or, at any rate, not widening, so that the bouquet is held and presented to your nostrils.

A glass of that shape that would hold a quarter-bottle of wine if filled to the very brim is ideal for any red or white table wine, and should be filled no more than half or two-thirds full at a time, so that there is room for the bouquet I have already mentioned.

Such a glass can be found at Woolworth's. Anything grander is self-indulgence.

Even self-indulgence, though, can be kept within bounds, and there are good glasses to be bought at only fifty or sixty pence apiece from Berry Brothers and from Justerini and Brooks, both in St James's Street, or by members from the Wine Society.

The same glass will do for champagne, though a taller, more slender, tulip shape shows off the bubble better. This sort of glass is also available at the St James's Street shops I mention, and at the same price as the other.

What one should *not* use – and here, for once, I shall be didactic – is the saucer-shaped glass, which the French call a

coupe. The shape is ugly in itself, for the bowl is disproportion-
ately wide for the height of the stem; it offers too much surface
of wine to the air, so that the fragrance is lost, and the bubbles
dissipated too quickly. It is a vulgar, silly glass, fit only for the
fancier confections of tinned fruits and factory-made ice-cream.

The only other glasses one needs in one's sideboard are
smaller versions of those I recommend for table wines, these
being for port and sherry. Better still for those wines, though,
and similarly available, is what is sometimes known as a dock
glass and in the sherry country itself as a *copita* – a glass rather
narrow for its height, and tapering towards the top.

This does well, too, for brandy, being small enough to be
cradled in the hand: the vast brandy balloons used in the sort of
restaurant that warms them over a spirit-lamp are suitable only
for the flashier sort of goldfish.

* * *

There may still be houses where the wine-glasses are the
personal responsibility of the butler, and appear gleaming on
the dinner-table, without ever a single smear or finger-mark or
wisp of lint from a drying-up cloth in a couple of dozen of
them. My own house, let me admit, is not one of them. We do
our best, but with hurried and amateur and too few hands, and
so, it seems, do most households and – with less excuse – many
hotels and restaurants.

It is not only a matter of appearance, though a table of
glittering glass looks splendid, whereas finger-marked glasses
look squalid, but a matter, too, of taste. A whiff of the washing-
up water will ruin a fine wine, and so can the smell of a glass
that is clinically clean, but has been too long upside-down in a
cupboard, catching and keeping a musty smell from the shelf
it has been sitting on.

The question now is, whether the newest washing-up devices
make things easier for the wine-lover, as they certainly do for
the washer-up, or whether they merely multiply the hazards
in the way of tasting wine at its best, and seeing it at its prettiest.

Champagne is the severest test of all, for its bubble as well as
its bouquet and flavour is at risk, and the London shippers of

Bollinger, having noticed at many big parties that champagne 'fell dead' as soon as it was poured into the glass, decided upon experiment.

They tried, with a selection of *grandes marques* champagne from Berry Brothers, four glasses that had been washed in detergent, and two washed in hot water without the aid of a detergent. Of the detergent-washed glasses, one was allowed to drain dry; one was dried with a cloth; one was rinsed in hot water and drain-dried; and one was rinsed in hot water and cloth-dried.

Only one of those washed in detergent came through successfully – the glass that had been rinsed afterwards in hot water, and dried with a clean cloth. The other three all affected the 'bubble', but in varying degrees – the most damaging being the glass that had been simply drain-dried. (One brand of detergent proved to be not quite so immediately lethal as another, but both were so damaging that there is no point in naming brands.) The two glasses washed without a detergent also came through the test with flying colours.

It is clear that even a speck of dried detergent left in the glass has a harmful effect – but the same is true of soap, or a drop of water. (Pour champagne into a perfectly clean but wet glass and see how the bubble dies.) My own experience with glasses washed with detergent in a washing-up machine that itself rinses in hot water as a final process is quite satisfactory. So use detergents, by all means, so long as you are sure that glasses are rinsed and cloth-dried afterwards: the same advice holds good for any other cleanser, and to wines other than champagne.

*   *   *

Is it worth while decanting wine? By all means. Fine, expensive old red wines need to be taken off the deposit that has formed in their bottles, and to be given the airing that will free them of 'bottle-stink' – air that has been trapped between cork, glass and wine for ten years or more is bound to smell.

Cheap young reds, too, are all the better for an airing. All very cheap wine is sold too young, for the profit margins all along the line between producer and consumer are too small to permit the grower's or the shipper's or the retailer's capital to be tied up in it while it matures.

I work at home, which means that I lunch and dine at home, seven days a week, and that means that we get through a good deal of what Liz calls swigging wine.

I try to buy Chilean and Tunisian and Moroccan reds (better value, to my mind, than the very cheapest French wines, from the Midi) enough at a time to give them another six months of bottle-age at home before drinking. In any case, I like to decant them into a carafe an hour or so before drinking – they have no deposit to be got rid of, but the airing of the stream of wine between bottle and carafe gives it a last-minute softening.

(The difference between a decanter and a carafe is that the decanter has a ground inside neck, and takes a stopper: a carafe does not.)

It is nice to have inherited fine Georgian decanters: twenty years or so ago one could buy them, in perfect condition, and with their original stoppers, for a couple of pounds apiece. In my bachelor days I used to buy them almost as fast as my cook-housekeeper could break them. Now, one pays twice as much, and more, for plain modern ones.

Decanting itself is easy.

Pour a young wine straight from bottle to decanter, but let an old wine stand upright for some hours in the dining-room so that while it takes on room temperature the deposit settles to the bottom of the bottle – in the groove round the punt, if it has one.

Then pour slowly, with the bottle between yourself and the light – ideally, with a candle-flame or small naked electric light-bulb behind the shoulder of the bottle.

A silver wine-funnel with a detachable strainer is a nice thing to have but not essential.

As soon as any muddy-looking deposit reaches the shoulder stop pouring. What is left goes into the kitchen for cooking and marinading, of which more anon from Liz.

Little bits of broken cork do no harm: cork is tasteless, or we would not keep our vintage ports and fine clarets lying for

years in the cellar deliberately with the wine touching the cork, to keep it moist.

So a fragment of cork in the glass does *not* mean that a wine is 'corked'. 'Corkiness' is a vile, fungus-like smell arising from a diseased cork – I think the disease is caused by some sort of grub. It is unmistakable, and it is so rare that you may never come across it in a lifetime of wine-drinking.

The practice of pouring the first few drops of wine into the host's glass is for him to smell it, and make sure that the wine is not corked – also so that any odd floating scraps of the cork are his and not his guests'.

Basket cradles are meant really for cellar use – to bring a bottle from bin to decanter without changing its angle too much. They should be used in restaurants only if the customer has given the wine-waiter no time to decant; only if the wine is old enough to have formed a deposit; and only if the wine-waiter pours as carefully from the bottle into each glass as into a decanter, and empties the bottle at one serving. Otherwise, if he ups and downs it to refill the glasses he is merely washing the deposit up and down and making quite sure that it is in suspension in everyone's glass.

Mostly, therefore, it is meaningless and unnecessary chichi.

White wine does not need decanting: the only deposit it throws, and that very rarely, is some little crystal-like flakes. They do no harm.

However, there are those cheap Italian carafes and the more expensive German jugs that I mentioned in an earlier chapter: they keep white wines cool at the table and, as all wine looks prettier in clear glass than in bottles, they are pleasant things to have.

The only corkscrew I care to use is the boxwood kind that has two handles – the small one at the top that screws in, and the bigger one, immediately below, that screws out. The bottle is upstanding all the time, and is not shaken about. I am a fool with my fingers, and this is foolproof.

Liz

I ensure a constant supply of wine for the kitchen by collecting what Ray leaves in the bottles he has decanted. The best way to do this is to keep two half-bottles – or, better still, a couple of the screw-top bottles that hold soda or tonic – one for red, the other for white. I suggest small bottles, as the less air space there is in the bottle the longer will the wine keep in good heart. (When I am doubtful about it and it seems tired or sour it goes into the vinegar bottle, as in chapter 6.) These bottles can be topped up with new nub-ends – a mixture of wines won't hurt for this purpose, and no one wants to go out and buy wine specially for cooking if there is some already in the house.

Wine adds richness to any number of dishes, both sweet and savoury, can be used with herbs and oil as a marinade, to tenderize and flavour dry meat; and a small amount added to the gravy of a plain roasted joint greatly enhances the flavour.

Dry cuts of meat, and game, both furred and feathered, especially benefit by being marinaded. A marinade is merely a bath for the meat, which soaks in an aromatic liquid for several hours, sometimes even days, then is sometimes cooked in the strained marinade, or taken from it and cooked plainly.

Some fish, too, especially fresh-water fish of the less exciting kind, benefit from this treatment, and herrings or mackerel soused, as mentioned in the chapter on white wines, are really marinaded, and cooked in the marinade.

Sometimes a marinade can be cooked first, as in the herring recipe I've just mentioned, or it can be a simple mixture of wine, oil and herbs.

The easiest and most straightforward method is to put the pieces of meat into a bowl and cover with red wine, oil, chopped onion and carrot, a bayleaf and any appropriate herb. Leave to soak for three or four hours, or even overnight, turning from time to time so that all pieces get the full treatment. One way is to see that the meat is in a deepish bowl, so that quite a small amount of marinade will cover it, or put the meat and liquid into a plastic bag (then put that into a bowl in case it leaks) and the same thing applies. If the meat is in a shallow dish, far more liquid is needed to cover it than is really necessary.

For an *estouffade* (French) or *stufato* (Italian) of beef – similar dishes, from different parts of the Mediterranean – a cooked marinade is often used. For this, heat a quarter-pint of oil, add a chopped carrot and onion, brown them in the oil, then add a quarter-pint of wine, red or white, and a dash of wine vinegar. Add a little garlic and parsley, some peppercorns and salt, and simmer for fifteen minutes or so. Cool, then pour over the meat and leave overnight. When the meat is ready to cook, take it out of the marinade, brown in fat, pour over the strained marinade, and cook in this, with more wine added if necessary, and some fresh vegetables, and cook, with the casserole closely covered, for about three hours, or until the meat is quite soft.

Afelia is a well-known family dish in Cyprus, and, like all family recipes, there are many ways of cooking it. But the basic ingredients of pork, red wine and coriander are the same, and mushrooms or small potatoes can be cooked the same way.

AFELIA

Cut about 1½lb of lean pork into inch and a half cubes, sprinkle with a tablespoon of roughly crushed coriander seeds, cover completely with a dry red wine and leave overnight or all day if the dish is to be cooked in the evening.

Strain off the wine, heat some oil and butter in a frying pan and sauté the pork pieces until they are lightly coloured. Add a glass of red wine to the pan, with a little water, season with salt and pepper and let the meat simmer gently until it is almost cooked and the liquid nearly absorbed. Add a good tablespoon of crushed coriander seeds and continue to cook for a few more minutes until the meat is completely tender. Traditionally, this should be served with a mash of crushed wheat, but here I think a rice pilaff, or mashed potatoes, would be the best accompaniment.

Pork, 1½lb; red wine, about ¾ bottle; oil, butter; salt; pepper; coriander seeds, 2 tablespoons

A delicious recipe, that comes from *The Flavour of France*, by the Chamberlains, is for:

MARINADED CARROTS

Scrape a pound of young carrots, cut them lengthways into quarters; put three-quarters of a cup of dry white wine, a cup of water, a bouquet garni, salt, pepper, two teaspoons of sugar, a crushed tooth of garlic and five tablespoons of olive oil into a saucepan, bring to the boil and simmer for five minutes. Add the carrots and boil them until almost done, but still firm. Let them cool in the liquid, then arrange them in a suitable dish and pour the liquid over them. Serve them cold, sprinkled with parsley, as part of an hors d'oeuvres.

Carrots, 1lb; white wine, ¾ cup; water, 1 cup; bouquet garni; salt; pepper; garlic; sugar; olive oil, 5 tablespoons

Here is a recipe that I haven't tried, and which may be too strong, but the ingredients are interesting, and I am told that if a leg of lamb or mutton is marinaded thus for a couple of days it tastes like venison.

Melt a tablespoon of redcurrant jelly, then add it to a quarter pint each of wine vinegar and port with a dash of Worcester sauce. Mix in a good seasoning of pepper, salt, chopped shallot or onion, and some thyme and marjoram.

In general, wine needs to be brought to boiling point at some time during any cooking process so that the alcohol evaporates whilst the flavour remains. If this doesn't happen, particularly with red wine, any sauce made with wine will have a raw unpleasant taste. The exceptions are in using such wines as sherry or Madeira in dishes where no cooking is involved, such as in syllabub or trifle.

The addition of a glass of wine to gravy, or in a sauce, however simple, will make an enormous difference. In general, use red wine for dark dishes and white for pale, not so much because of the difference to the taste, but because, while a white wine will not alter the colour of a brown sauce, a red wine will make a pale sauce look unpleasantly muddy.

Although marinades usually contain wine, there are some dishes that are marinaded without, in order to give them a particular flavour, or to preserve them in some way. One is this recipe for *Gravlax* – a Swedish dish meaning Buried Salmon, an excellent way of treating salmon, which makes it good to eat raw, but quite different from smoked salmon.

GRAVLAX

Take 2lb of middle-cut salmon, split it lengthways and remove the backbone. Wipe and dry the fish, and put one half skin-side down into a dish and sprinkle with a mixture of four tablespoons of chopped dill, two tablespoons of sugar, the same amount of coarse salt, and a teaspoon of ground white pepper. Place the other half of the fish on top, skin-side up, putting the broad end of the top piece of fish to the thin end of the underneath bit. Cover with foil or greaseproof paper, then with a weighted dish, and leave in a cool place for at least 24 hours, preferably for two days.

During this time, baste the salmon once or twice with the liquid that forms (not forgetting to baste the inside, too). When the *gravlax* is ready separate the halves, pat them dry and put skin-side down on a serving dish and garnish with lemon. Slice very thinly, as for smoked salmon, and serve a mustardy sauce with it. This is made by mixing two tablespoons of French or German mustard with a teaspoon of mustard powder, two tablespoons of sugar, two tablespoons of vinegar, four tablespoons of oil and some chopped dill.

Salmon, 2lb; dill, 4 tablespoons; sugar, 2 tablespoons; salt, 2 tablespoons; pepper, 1 teaspoon

For the sauce: Mixed mustard (French or German), 2 tablespoons; mustard powder, 1 teaspoon; sugar, 2 tablespoons; vinegar; 2 tablespoons; oil, 4 tablespoons; chopped dill

MARINADED KIPPER FILLETS

Mix together three or four tablespoons of oil with the juice of half a lemon, and season with black pepper.

Pour this over four or six kipper fillets, leave for two or three hours, turning once or twice.

Drain the fillets of the oil and serve with brown bread and butter and lemon like smoked salmon.

Kipper fillets, 4–6; lemon, $\frac{1}{2}$; oil, 3–4 tablespoons; black pepper

BIRIYANI

Marinade 1lb diced lean lamb in half a carton of natural yogurt and a heaped tablespoon of curry powder for two hours.

Fry a chopped onion in oil, then remove it and place in a casserole. Fry the meat in the same pan for about three minutes, then remove it and add to the onion. Still using the same pan, put in a pint of stock and add two large potatoes, peeled and diced, and bring to the boil. Sprinkle in two ounces of patna rice and simmer for 10 minutes.

Add an ounce of sultanas and pour the vegetables and stock over the lamb in the casserole, season with salt, cover

and cook for an hour in a moderate (350° gas 3) oven. Sprinkle with an ounce of toasted flaked almonds before serving.

Lamb, 1lb; yogurt, ½ carton; curry powder, 1 tablespoon; onion, 1; oil for frying; stock, 1 pint; potatoes, 2; rice, 2oz; sultanas, 1 oz; salt; almonds, 1oz

One addition to Ray's advice on glasses and decanters – I have found that the easiest way to clean decanters which are wine stained is to put in a Steradent tablet, fill with hot water, leave for a quarter of an hour or so, then rinse thoroughly, and the stain will have gone. Much easier than the old way of using torn-up newspaper or shot, less harmful to the glass, and less likely to taste than the bleach that I have seen recommended.

Appendices

WEIGHTS AND MEASURES

A convenient method of converting recipe quantities is to round off gramme and millilitre measurements to the nearest unit of 25. The charts below give the exact conversion (to the nearest whole figure) of Imperial ounces and fluid ounces to grammes and millilitres, and the recommended equivalent based on the nearest unit of 25.

Solid measures

Ounces	Grammes	Recommended equivalent to nearest 25
1	28	25
2	57	50
3	85	75
4	113	100
5	142	150
6	170	175
7	198	200
8 (½lb)	226	225
12 (¾lb)	340	350
16 (1lb)	456	450

Liquid measures

Fluid ounces	Millilitres to nearest whole figure	Recommended equivalent to nearest 25
1	28	25
2	57	50
3	85	75
4	113	100 (1 decilitre)
5 ($\frac{1}{4}$ pint)	142	150
6	170	175
7	198	200 (2 decilitres)
8	226	225
9	255	250
10 ($\frac{1}{2}$ pint)	283	275
15 ($\frac{3}{4}$ pint)	428	425
20 (1 pint)	569	575

When converting quantities over 1lb or 1 pint, add together the appropriate figures in the centre column (the direct conversion) before rounding off to the nearest unit of 25.

Note on metric units of measurement: 1 litre (1000 millilitres, 10 decilitres) equals 1.76 pints, or almost exactly $1\frac{3}{4}$ pints. 1 kilogramme (1000 grammes) equals 2.2 pounds, or almost exactly 2 pounds 3 ounces.

OVEN TEMPERATURES

The chart below gives the conversions from degrees Fahrenheit to degrees Celsius (formerly referred to as Centigrade) recommended by the manufacturers of electric cookers.

	Fahrenheit setting	Recommended C. setting	Gas Mark
Very cool	225	110	$\frac{1}{4}$
	250	130	$\frac{1}{2}$
Cool	275	140	1
	300	150	2
Very moderate	325	170	3
Moderate	350	180	4
	375	190	5
Moderately hot	400	200	6
Hot	425	220	7
	450	230	8
Very hot	475	240	9

Index

Recipes are shown in bold type; an asterisk (*) indicates that a food recipe includes wine; a dagger (†) indicates a recipe for a concocted beverage.